Building
Jerusalem

Building Jerusalem

Elegies on Parish Churches

*Edited with
an introduction by*

Kevin J. Gardner

B L O O M S B U R Y

LONDON • OXFORD • NEW YORK • NEW DELHI • SYDNEY

Bloomsbury Continuum

An imprint of Bloomsbury Publishing Plc

50 Bedford Square   1385 Broadway
London   New York
WC1B 3DP   NY 10018
UK   USA

www.bloomsbury.com

**Bloomsbury, Continuum and the Diana logo are trademarks
of Bloomsbury Publishing Plc**

First published 2016

© Kevin J. Gardner, 2016

British Library Cataloguing-in-Publication Data
A catalogue record for this book is available from the British Library.

ISBN: HB: 978-1-4729-2435-3
ePDF: 978-1-4729-2437-7
ePub: 978-1-4729-2436-0

2 4 6 8 10 9 7 5 3 1

Printed and bound in Great Britain by CPI Group (UK) Ltd, Croydon CR0 4YY

To find out more about our authors and books visit www.bloomsbury.com.
Here you will find extracts, author interviews, details of forthcoming
events and the option to sign up for our newsletters.

For rigorous teachers seized my youth,
And purged its faith, and trimmed its fire,
Showed me the high, white star of Truth,
There bade me gaze, and there aspire.
Even now their whispers pierce the gloom:
What dost thou in this living tomb?

MATTHEW ARNOLD,
Stanzas from the Grande Chartreuse, ll. 67–72

Contents

Preface

Compiling this anthology began in solitude and ended in collaboration. Even working in silence I was never alone, for I kept the company of poets: their images and rhythms were my taciturn companions. In time, of course, the solitude gave way to a host of welcome voices who contributed in vital ways to this anthology, and to each of them I am extraordinarily grateful. By the time this collection was complete, I had benefited from the gracious support and assistance of many individuals and had thus amassed a vast and unpayable debt of obligation. In remembering these, I apologise to any I may have forgotten.

First, I must thank the poets themselves, for writing the profound and lovely works that comprise this volume, and for their imaginative attention to Britain's living and dying churches. I wish especially to thank Anthony Thwaite, Peter Scupham, Neil Powell and Tony Connor. I deeply treasure the friendships I have developed with them and their encouragement of my research and writing. I have had many delightful exchanges with them on the subject of writing and reading poetry. I am particularly appreciative of their advice on this project and eternally grateful for their generosity in contributing so many of their poems to this collection and sharing the stories of their poems with me.

In researching and compiling this anthology it has been my great good fortune to have made the acquaintance of many other poets as well: Fleur Adcock, Simon Armitage, Glen Cavaliero, Gillian Clarke, Kevin Crossley-Holland, Roger Garfitt, John Greening, Michael Henry, Brian Hinton, Jeremy Hooker, P.J. Kavanagh, Hubert Moore, Andrew Motion, Rodney Pybus, Anne Stevenson, Seán Street, Kim Taplin, Andrew Waterman and Clive Wilmer. I am grateful for their generous responses to my queries and for providing helpful background on their poems. I wish to thank them for their letters and emails, for their support of this project, and for their permission to include their work in this anthology.

My gratitude extends as well to those poets who have died, and I am indebted to those who serve as their literary executors: Annabella Ashby (for Cliff Ashby), Dr R.V. Bailey (for U.A. Fanthorpe), Elspeth Barker (for George Barker), Susan Bassnett (for Anne Cluysenaar), Rian Evans (for John Ormond), Christine Faunch and Sue Inskip of the University of Exeter Special Collections (for Jack Clemo), John Fuller (for Roy Fuller), Roger Garfitt (for Frances Horovitz), Deirdre Connolly Levi (for Peter Levi), Matthew Lomas (for Bertie Lomas), Ruth Lowbury (for Andrew Young), Glyn Mathias (for Roland Mathias), Christine Porter (for Peter Porter) and Martin Reed (for Vernon Scannell). These executors wrote letters and emails in support of this project, and I am grateful to them for the generous permission they extended to reprint the work of those whose estates they represent.

A number of others have offered advice, encouragement or assistance. Biographer, historian and critic Bevis Hillier read my manuscript and offered invaluable criticism, particularly of the Introduction; over the years I have learned much about writing from him, and his frequent emails sustained me with his wit while I compiled this anthology. Michael Schmidt, editor of *PN Review*, read my proposal; his enthusiasm for this project in its early stages was of singular importance. Luke Thompson, PhD candidate at Exeter, gave long and thoughtful responses to my queries about Jack Clemo and Geoffrey Grigson. Simon Knott's 'The Churches of East Anglia', an Internet collection, proved extraordinarily helpful. Vital advice and assistance was also provided by David Sutton of the University of Reading, editor of the WATCH Files; Sarah Baxter of the Society of Authors; Helena Nelson, founder and editor of Happenstance Press; Maryam Piracha, editor of *The Missing Slate*; Martin Malone, editor of *The Interpreter's House*; Mick Felton, publisher of Seren Books; and my Baylor colleague, Richard R. Russell. Additional thanks are due to Matthew Connolly, Charlie Louth, Mark Jackson, John R. Murray, Philip Payton and Michael J. Collins.

I am grateful as well to the following literary agents, publishers and rights managers, for their assistance with licensing agreements to reprint copyrighted material: Georgia Glover at David Higham Associates; Rosie Price at Rogers, Coleridge & White; Sharon Rubin at Peters Fraser & Dunlop; Philippa Sitters at David Godwin Associates; Tony Ward at Arc Publications; Caroline White at Tabb House Books; John Lucas and Nathanael Ravenlock at Shoestring Press; Stephen Stuart-Smith and Peter Target at Enitharmon Press; Michael Schmidt, Michelle Healey and Christine Steel at Carcanet Press; Peter Jay at Anvil Press Poetry; Neil Astley and Suzanne Fairless-Aitken at Bloodaxe Books; Tom Atkins at Random House; Maya Kayukwa at Hodder & Stoughton; Devon Mazzone and Victoria Fox at Farrar, Straus and Giroux; Beverley Gadsden, Quentin Huon and Simon Darlington-Crammond at Macmillan; Hannah Goodman at Orion; Donna Anstey of Yale University Press; and Alex Bradshaw, Luke Edwards and Ineke Stevenson at Penguin.

I am deeply appreciative of many friends and colleagues at Baylor University who offered assistance and support. This project was supported in part by funds from the Baylor University Research Committee and the Vice Provost for Research. I should like to thank Dr Truell Hyde, Vice Provost for Research, and the staff of the Office of Sponsored Programs, for their assistance in helping me to secure a University Research Grant to support this project, without which it is unlikely that it could have been completed. I would like to recognize Interlibrary Services at Moody Memorial Library for facilitating an inordinate number of my requests to borrow books. Finally, I would like to thank my colleagues in the Department of English for their interest in this project and their encouragement of my research.

For the kindness and assistance of so many people at Bloomsbury Continuum in ushering this book into print, I have a long list of thanks as well. I am especially grateful to publishing director Robin Baird-Smith, for his long-standing support of my work, and for his enthusiasm for this project in particular, when so many other editors doubted its success. Jamie Birkett worked tirelessly with me in ensuring that the book was properly edited and designed. The beautiful jacket design is owing to the remarkable vision of Sutchinda Thompson. Copyeditor Emily Sweet and proofreader Catherine Best were exceptionally effective in their attention to detail. Additionally, I should like to acknowledge Sarah Lewis and Richard Johnston for their assistance.

Finally, my profound gratitude is due to the Churches Conservation Trust, the Friends of Friendless Churches, the National Churches Trust and other organizations committed to preserving Britain's ecclesiastical fabric. I must acknowledge my friend and mentor Joseph Roach, whose book *Cities of the Dead*, if memory serves, introduced me to the pattern of remembering and forgetting as literary motif and cultural practice. And most importantly, it has been the greatest fortune to have the love and encouragement of my wife, Hilary, and my son, Graham. To them I dedicate this volume.

Acknowledgements

Every effort has been made to contact the copyright holders of the poems that comprise this collection. In the case of oversight, the copyright holder is encouraged to contact the publisher so that appropriate arrangements may be made. The editor and publisher would like to make the following acknowledgements for permission to reproduce copyrighted material: 'At Great Hampden' and 'Kilpeck' appear in *Poems 1960–2000* by Fleur Adcock (Bloodaxe, 2000) and are reproduced by kind permission of Bloodaxe Books and the author. 'Harmonium' is taken from *Paper Aeroplane: Selected Poems 1989–2014* copyright © Simon Armitage and is reprinted by kind permission of Faber & Faber Ltd, of David Godwin Associates, and the author. 'Rains' appears in *Risings* by Peter Armstrong (Enitharmon, 1988) and is reprinted by kind permission of Enitharmon Press. 'Fountains Abbey' appears in *Plain Song: Collected Poems* (Carcanet, 1985) and is reprinted by kind permission of Annabella Ashby on behalf of the Estate of Cliff Ashby. 'The Angels of Muchelney', published originally in *The Interpreter's House*, vol. 49, is used by kind permission of the author, Juliet Aykroyd. 'At Thurgarton Church' appears in *Collected Poems* by George Barker (Faber & Faber, 1987) and is reprinted by kind permission of Elspeth Barker on behalf of the Estate of George Barker. 'A Lincolnshire Church', 'St Saviour's, Aberdeen Park, Highbury, London, N.', 'Sunday Morning, King's Cambridge' and 'Uffington' appear in *Collected Poems* by John Betjeman (John Murray, 2006) and are reprinted by kind permission of Hodder & Stoughton and the Estate of Sir John Betjeman. 'At St Hilary' and 'St Protus & St Hyacinth, Blisland' appear in *Collected Poems 1951–2000* by Charles Causley (Picador, 2000) and are reprinted by kind permission of the Estate of Charles Causley and of Picador. 'Fenland Churches' appears in *The Ancient People* by Glen Cavaliero (Carcanet, 1973) and is reprinted by kind permission of the author. 'A Redundant Church' appears in *Paradise Stairway* by Glen Cavaliero (Carcanet, 1977) and is reprinted by kind permission of the author. 'Top Church' is used by kind permission of the author, Gillian Clarke; an earlier version of this poem appears in *Collected Poems* (Carcanet, 1997) under the title 'St Augustine's, Penarth'. 'In Roche Church' appears in *A Different Drummer* by Jack Clemo (Tabb House, 1986) and is reprinted by kind permission of Tabb House, Padstow, Cornwall. 'About the Church' appears in *Timeslips: New and Selected Poems* by Anne Cluysenaar (Carcanet, 1997) and is reprinted by kind permission of Susan Bassnett and Walter Jackson on behalf of the Estate of Anne Cluysenaar. 'St Mark's, Cheetham Hill' appears in *Things Unsaid: Selected Poems 1960–2005* by Tony Connor (Anvil Press Poetry, 2006) and is reproduced by kind permission of the author and the publisher. 'In Luss Churchyard' appears in *Collected Poems* by Iain Crichton Smith (Carcanet, 1995) and is reprinted by kind permission of Carcanet Press, Ltd. 'Angels at St Mary's' appears in *Poems from East Anglia* by Kevin Crossley-Holland (Enitharmon, 1997) and is reprinted with kind permission of the author and of Enitharmon Press. 'In Latter Days' appears in *The Language of Yes* by Kevin Crossley-Holland (Enitharmon, 1996) and is reprinted by kind permission of the author and of Enitharmon Press. 'Leaving Towcester Vicarage' appears in *Comet Over Greens Norton: New and Selected Poems* by Simon Curtis (Shoestring Press, 2013) and is reprinted by kind permission of

Shoestring Press. 'The Priory of St Saviour, Glendalough' appears in *Collected Poems* by Donald Davie (Carcanet, 2002) and is reprinted by kind permission of Carcanet Press, Ltd. 'Seen From the Train' is from *The Complete Poems* by Cecil Day-Lewis, published by Sinclair Stevenson, 1992, reproduced by permission of The Random House Group, Ltd. 'Greensted Church', 'St James, Charfield', and '"Soothing and Awful"' are reprinted from U.A. Fanthorpe, *New and Collected Poems* (Enitharmon Press, 2010), with the kind permission of Dr R.V. Bailey, © Estate of U.A. Fanthorpe. 'Youth Revisited' appears in *Selected Poems* by Roy Fuller (Carcanet, 2012) and is reprinted by kind permission of Carcanet Press, Ltd, and of John Fuller on behalf of the Estate of Roy Fuller. 'Rites of Passage' is used by kind permission of the author, Roger Garfitt; an earlier version appeared in *Given Ground* (Carcanet, 1989), and subsequently in the poetry magazine *Planet* in 2012. 'A Huntingdonshire Elegy' and 'A Huntingdonshire Nocturne' appear in *Hunts: Poems 1979–2009* by John Greening (Greenwich Exchange, 2009) and are reprinted by kind permission of the author. 'West Window' appears in *Collected Poems 1963–1980* by Geoffrey Grigson (Allison & Busby, 1982) and is reprinted by kind permission of the Estate of Geoffrey Grigson and of Allison & Busby. 'Churchyard of Saint Mary Magdalene, Old Milton' appears in *Selected Poems* by John Heath-Stubbs (Carcanet, 1990) and is reprinted by kind permission of the Estate of John Heath-Stubbs and of Carcanet Press. 'St Martin in the Field' appears in *Panto Sphinx* by Michael Henry (Enitharmon, 1991) and is reprinted by kind permission of the author and of Enitharmon Press. 'Slipper Chapel' appears in *An Ocean in My Ear* by Michael Henry (Enitharmon, 1988) and is reprinted by kind permission of the author and of Enitharmon Press. 'Epiphany at Saint Mary and All Saints' is taken from *Without Title* by Geoffrey Hill (Penguin/Yale, 2006) and is reprinted by kind permission of the Penguin Group, London, and of Yale University Press. 'Loss and Gain' is part of a sequence of thirteen poems entitled *An Apology for the Revival of Christian Architecture in England*, published originally in *Tenebrae* by Geoffrey Hill (André Deutsch, 1978); it appears in *Selected Poems* by Geoffrey Hill (Penguin, 2006) and is reprinted by kind permission of the Penguin Group, London. 'All Saints' appears in *The Heart's Clockwork* by Brian Hinton (Enitharmon, 1989) and is reprinted by kind permission of the author and of Enitharmon Press. 'St Cross' appears in *Master of the Leaping Figures* by Jeremy Hooker (Enitharmon, 1987) and is reprinted by kind permission of the author and of Enitharmon Press. 'Country Afternoon' is from *Collected Poems* by Frances Horovitz (Bloodaxe, 1989) and is reproduced by kind permission of Bloodaxe Books and of Roger Garfitt on behalf of the Estate of Frances Horovitz. 'Heptonstall Old Church' is taken from *Collected Poems* © Estate of Ted Hughes and is reprinted by kind permission of Faber & Faber Ltd and of Farrar, Straus and Giroux, LLC. 'Somerset' appears in *The Collected Poems* by Elizabeth Jennings (Carcanet, 2012) and is reprinted by kind permission of the Estate of Elizabeth Jennings and of Carcanet Press. 'Westwell Churchyard, Oxfordshire' appears in *New Selected Poems* by P.J. Kavanagh (Carcanet, 2014) and is reprinted by kind permission of the author and of Carcanet Press, Ltd. 'Church Going' and 'A Stone Church Damaged by a Bomb' are taken from *Collected Poems* © Estate of Philip Larkin and are reprinted by kind permission of Faber & Faber Ltd and of Farrar, Straus and Giroux, LLC. 'Shobdon' appears in *Reed Music* by Peter Levi (Anvil Press Poetry, 1997) and is used by kind permission of the publisher and of Deirdre Connolly Levi on behalf of the Estate of Peter Levi. 'Christ Church' and 'St Martin-in-the-Fields' appear in *A Casual Knack of Living: Collected Poems* by Herbert Lomas (Arc, 2009) and are reprinted by kind permission of Arc Publications and of Matthew Lomas on behalf of the Estate of Herbert Lomas. 'Brechfa Chapel' appears in *Collected Poems* by Roland Mathias (University of Wales

Press, 2002) and is reprinted by kind permission of Glyn Mathias on behalf of the Estate of Roland Mathias. 'Crossing the Church' appears in *Rolling Stock* by Hubert Moore (Enitharmon, 1991) and is reprinted by kind permission of the author and of Enitharmon Press. 'For Now', published originally in the *Guardian*, is used by kind permission of the author, Sir Andrew Motion. 'Of this Parish' appears in *Collected Poems* by Norman Nicholson (Faber & Faber, 1994) and is reprinted by kind permission of the Estate of Norman Nicholson and of Faber & Faber. 'Cathedral Builders' appears in *Collected Poems* by John Ormond (Seren Books, 2015) and is reprinted by kind permission of Rian Evans on behalf of the Estate of John Ormond. 'An Angel in Blythburgh Church' and 'At Whitechurch Canonicorum' appear in *Collected Poems: Vol. 1, 1961–1981* by Peter Porter (Oxford, 1983, reissued 1999) and are reprinted by kind permission of Mrs Christine Porter and of Rogers, Coleridge & White Literary Agency. 'The Rider Haggard Window, St Mary's, Ditchingham' appears in *The Rest on the Flight: Selected Poems* by Peter Porter (Picador, 2010), copyright © Peter Porter, 2004, and is reprinted by kind permission of Mrs Christine Porter and of Pan Macmillan Publishers. 'At Little Gidding', 'Iken', 'Leiston Abbey' and 'Providence' appear in *Selected Poems* by Neil Powell (Carcanet, 1998) and are reprinted by kind permission of the author and of Carcanet Press, Ltd. 'Suffolk Church' appears in *Cicadas in Their Summers* by Ronald Pybus (Carcanet, 1988) and is reprinted by kind permission of the author. 'Boveney Church' appears in *Selected Poems* by Vicki Raymond (Carcanet, 1993) and is reprinted by kind permission of Carcanet Press, Ltd. 'St James's' appears in *Collected Poems, vol. 1: 1970–1984* by Peter Reading (Bloodaxe, 1995) and is reproduced by kind permission of Bloodaxe Books. 'Edlesborough' appears in *Collected Poems* by Anne Ridler (Carcanet, 1997) and is reprinted by kind permission of Carcanet Press, Ltd. 'In a City Churchyard' appears in *Collected Poems 1950–1993* by Vernon

Scannell (Robson Books, 1993) and is reprinted by kind permission of
Martin Reed on behalf of the Estate of Vernon Scannell. 'Locking the
Church' appears in *Beyond the Drift: New & Selected Poems* by David
Scott (Bloodaxe, 2015) and is reprinted by kind permission of Bloodaxe
Books. 'Dissolution', 'Minsden', 'Rule', 'Service' and 'Stone Head' appear
in *Collected Poems* by Peter Scupham (Carcanet, 2002) and are
reprinted by kind permission of the author and of Carcanet Press, Ltd.
'In Kent', 'Knole' and 'Muchelney Abbey' appear in *Collected Poems* by
C.H. Sisson (Carcanet, 1998) and are reprinted by kind permission of
Carcanet Press, Ltd. 'At the Church of St John Baptist, Preston Bissett,
May 1974' appears in *Rounding the Horn: Collected Poems* by Jon
Stallworthy (Carcanet, 1998) and is reprinted by kind permission of
Carcanet Press, Ltd. 'Pennine' appears in *Poems 1955–2005* by Anne
Stevenson (Bloodaxe, 2005) and is reproduced by kind permission of
Bloodaxe Books and the author. 'Churchyard' appears in *Time Between
Tides* by Seán Street (Rockingham Press, 2009) and is reprinted by
kind permission of the author and the publisher. 'Knowlton, Cranborne
Chase' appears in *A Walk in Winter* (Enitharmon, 1989) and is
reprinted by kind permission of the author and of Enitharmon Press.
'Fairford Windows' is one in a sequence of ten poems published first as
Muniments (Jackson's Arm, 1987) and reprinted in *By the Harbour
Wall* (Enitharmon, 1990) and is reproduced by kind permission of
Enitharmon Press and the author, Kim Taplin. 'The Belfry' and
'Country Church (Manafon)' are taken from *Collected Poems 1945–
1990* © R.S. Thomas, 1993, and are reprinted by kind permission of
Orion Publishing Group, London. 'At Dunkeswell Abbey', 'At Dunwich',
'Eccles', 'Manhood End', 'The Mole at Kilpeck Church' and 'Reformation'
appear in *Collected Poems* by Anthony Thwaite (Enitharmon, 2007)
and are reprinted by kind permission of the author and of Enitharmon
Press. 'Ludham, St Catherine's Church, The Rood Screen' appears in
Collected Poems 1959–1999 by Andrew Waterman (Carcanet, 2000)

and is reprinted by kind permission of the author and of Carcanet Press, Ltd. 'Please Close This Door Quietly' appears in *The Other Mountain* by Rowan Williams (Carcanet, 2014) and is reprinted by kind permission of Carcanet Press, Ltd. 'East Anglian Churchyard', 'Near Walsingham' and 'The Ruined Abbey' appear in *New and Collected Poems* by Clive Wilmer (Carcanet, 2012) and are reprinted by kind permission of the author and of Carcanet Press, Ltd. 'The Ruined Chapel' appears in *Selected Poems* by Andrew Young (Carcanet, 1998) and is reprinted by kind permission of Carcanet Press, Ltd.

Introduction

Anglican Memory and Post-War British Poetry

In Philip Larkin's famous poem 'Church Going', the speaker surreptitiously penetrates old churches in a state not of devotion but of architectural, historical and cultural curiosity. Entering an empty church in 'awkward reverence', as if the remembrance of a formerly spiritual life survives somewhere within himself, he mounts the lectern and utters a familiar phrase, 'Here endeth', the lector's response to the reading of the lessons. These words evoke no memories of forgotten scripture but instead simply forecast the end of belief. Though an inveterate church-crawler, the speaker pretends not to understand the 'brass and stuff / Up at the holy end', yet his knowledge of arcane ecclesial artefacts (the pyx, the rood-loft) suggests that the memory of Anglican ritual is well preserved. The whole experience saddens this 'ruin-bibber' but not because of a personal loss of spirituality; instead, two other losses are to blame. The first of these is the abandonment of church buildings to uncertain future uses: 'wondering, too, / When churches fall completely out of use / What we shall turn them into'. The second is the ignorance of the common English people of their historical faith and its displacement by superstition: 'after dark, will dubious women come / To make their children touch a particular stone; / Pick simples for a cancer; or on some / Advised night see walking a dead one?' The poet laments the loss of communal faith and religious ritual, a loss which he attempts to recuperate by reminding us of the significance of church buildings: a church is a 'serious house' to which people will now and again be magnetically drawn because seriousness is a fundamental human quality: 'And that much never can be obsolete, / Since someone will forever be surprising / A hunger in himself to be more serious, / And gravitating with it to this ground.'

The defining aspect of post-war Britain in this monumental poem is the loss of a cohesive cultural identity once sustained by a common faith. To Larkin, though himself a non-believer, the widespread loss of Anglican memory is a cultural tragedy that bespeaks an ethical void within British society, a void exacerbated in the decades following the Second World War by a collective and prevailing climate of resignation and malaise. Historian George Lichtheim eloquently captures the sense of ennui and frustration of a nation unable to define itself:

> Those who have the melancholy privilege of living in the capital of what was once the British Empire ... have come to know well the feeling that greatness is gone and meanness has come in: meanness of spirit consequent upon the relentless decline of material influence and power, for it is an illusion to suppose that nations can sublimate themselves into moral entities impervious to the march of history.[1]

Lichtheim's dismissal of the fantasy of a nation as a moral entity has direct bearing on a state with an established Church. This was because the aim of the Church of England was not simply to be the state-approved manifestation of Christianity in England but to be the spiritual embodiment of the English people. As Stephen Neill, an

---

[1]'Post-Imperial Britain', *Commentary*, October 1966, p. 71.

Anglican bishop and theologian, suggests, the purpose of Anglicanism is as much communal as spiritual; its aim is 'to gather into one all those whom God had united as members of a single nation'.[2] (Of course, such a definition ignores an important historical reality: the Church of England was born in schism and nursed in carnage.)

The idea of a spiritually unified people must have seemed especially preposterous in the years following the Second World War, as the Church of England began to witness a precipitous decline in regular attendance as well as in the identification of English people as Anglicans. With sizeable demographic shifts and church attendance in freefall following the war, the Church Commissioners developed a scheme to shed its redundant and decaying churches. Particularly in urban areas, the property value of a church's site was often seen as greater than its spiritual or architectural value, and thus many buildings were sold off and demolished. Since the 1950s thousands of parish churches have been declared redundant and closed, and the trend continues to this day. Weekly attendance in the Church of England amounts to less than 2 per cent of the population, and no alternative collective cultural identification has filled the void. Yet the Church's potency is not entirely gone: the longing for ritual manages to draw a significant number of English people back into the parish church for baptism, marriage and funerals. The surprising increase in religiosity at these three signal events in human life (hatching, matching and dispatching, as an old Anglican joke puts it) suggests that Anglican memory runs deep in the bone. Despite these ritual homecomings, however, no one could deny that the Church of England is moribund and that its power over ordinary lives is insignificant.

What survives of Anglicanism, then, is not so much the faith but the fabric of the faith – the 35,000 or more parish churches that

---

[2]*Anglicanism* (Harmondsworth, UK: Penguin, 1958), p. 426.

adorn the landscape of England's green and pleasant land. While many of these still thrive as spaces of living worship, countless others barely cling to life. The post-war Church's heedless disregard of its own heritage only reinforced the widespread lassitude of the English people towards their historic environment and culture. Among the most vocal and active critics of that course of indifference was John Betjeman, whose particular gift was an ability to tap successfully into the collective imagination of the English. Here Betjeman recollects a landscape whose beauty is dependent upon and made complete by old parish churches:

> Lichen-crested granite towers appearing above wind-slashed Cornish elms, smoke coming from the boiler-house chimney on a Saturday afternoon when the stove has been lit for to-morrow's service: noble stone towers and spires in hunting country of the Midlands: huge East Anglian fanes of flint and glass, with angel roofs inside them, old benches, crumbling screens and pale plastered walls: sturdy fortress-like churches of the north: Greek temples in the older industrial towns, and insistent through the roar of the traffic the tinkle from Tudor turrets or Renaissance steeples of bells calling to cedarwood altar pieces: brass chandeliers and ironwork recalling Lord Mayors and Aldermen and civic splendour: red-tiled church roofs of Kent and Sussex which glow like autumn fires above flint and stone walls: no country in the world has such a rich variety of old churches as England.[3]

Betjeman's instinct to preserve endangered churches was about spiritual as well as aesthetic conservation. Those driven by fiscal motives to shutter churches 'forget that a church as a building is a

---

[3]'The Fabric of Our Faith', *Punch*, 23 December 1953, p. 744.

more lasting witness to our Christian faith than any bishop, vicar, churchwarden or congregation. A civilization is remembered and judged by her buildings. That is why every church, however remote and, maybe only temporarily, unsuccessful, must be kept in repair and open and alive.' In an argument that unites English myth-making with Christian faith, Betjeman insists that churches must be saved, 'If we have any faith left, any love of what makes England beautiful and England for us.' Thus Betjeman urged the English to remember the cultural, social and spiritual value of threatened churches – and to contribute financially to their preservation.

But for a few outspoken individuals and several well-organized preservation societies, the apathy and destruction might have continued unchecked. Eventually the vision of Betjeman and the value of preserving historic spaces of worship became widely embraced, and it is now generally accepted that when historic churches must be closed they should be saved and reconstituted for alternative purposes. Whether abandoned or in use, however, the churches of England now serve largely as memorials to lost belief and lost ritual. To French historian Pierre Nora, the modern world is typified by such *lieux de mémoire*, sites of collective memory fragmented and preserved apart from the flow of history, neither quite dead nor quite alive. Such places of memory are 'like shells on the shore when the sea of living memory has receded'.[4] Indeed, churches remain in the English landscape as monuments of living memory, revenants of an era of belief and ritual. From such a perspective, the Church can be seen as embodying the history of England; it is a place of cultural remembrance. For Simon Jenkins, journalist and former chairman of the National Trust (and an admitted agnostic), churches serve 'as witness to the bonds that

---

[4]'Between Memory and History: *Les Lieux de Mémoire*', *Representations*, 26 (Spring 1989), p. 12.

have brought the English people together in village and town through a thousand years of history'. To Jenkins this is cause for both comfort and alarm: 'It is through the churches of England that we learn who we were and thus who we are and might become. Lose that learning and we lose the collective memory that is the essence of human society. We must remember.'[5] The remembrance of this once significant institution has been taken up by the poet, for whom the passing of the Church into collective memory is cause for elegiac lament. One need not be a believer to express the *ubi sunt* motif of Anglicanism. To the agnostic as well as the devout, the need to remember what is almost forgotten has remained a powerful poetic urge. What makes church elegies interesting is not so much their exploration of the contours of belief and doubt as their probing of the interstices of consciousness and recollection. The poet transforms into a work of art the cycle of forgetting and remembering, and thus lamenting a lost world of faith recuperates the collective memory of Anglicanism.

Of course, Anglicanism is not some sort of cultural glue that holds together a fragmented English culture; indeed, post-war cultural identity is relentlessly incoherent and multivalent. Nevertheless, many poets, seeking that very glue, have found it in the Church – or more accurately within the collective memory of the Church. Anglican worship is, however, a communal experience and occurs within specified architectural spaces – sites of memory that give a social shape and order to individual impulses – and thus the memorial appeal of the established Church to those fretted by the disorder, fragmentation and amnesia of modern society. In a sense, then, a form of cultural identity may be discovered in the voices of poets who lament the loss of Anglicanism as a system that once united the English in thought and custom: the celebration of memory transposed by forgetting. This

---

[5]*England's Thousand Best Churches* (London: Allen Lane, 1999), p. xxix.

phenomenon typifies the work of a significant number of post-war English poets – believers as well as agnostics; Anglicans, Catholics, Nonconformists and Jews – whose work might be considered jointly as an effort to restore a common identity by way of recollecting a forgotten Anglican culture. These poets are diverse in voice, form and belief; what unites this polyphonous group is that in decrying cultural amnesia and fragmentation they steep themselves in the collective memory of Anglicanism as a form of cultural identity. As their poems demonstrate, churches and churchyards are to be commemorated as sites of cultural identity and collective memory: they endow the history and landscape of Britain with a Christian mythology, lament the social and political ramifications of a post-Christian culture, and remember and recoup the remains of lost belief. Kim Taplin succinctly expresses this loss in her poem 'Sunday': 'there's always a church-shaped hole in your life somewhere'.[6]

The phenomenon of the church elegy came to prominence in the 1950s with the widespread popularity of Philip Larkin and John Betjeman. The chords their poems struck resonated with numerous poets in subsequent decades, and by my count at least two hundred marvellous and profound poems have been written on the subject in the last sixty or seventy years. Perhaps the most prolific of church elegists in recent years have been Anthony Thwaite, Peter Scupham and Neil Powell.[7] In a published interview, Powell elicits an amusing anecdote from Scupham: 'I remember Anthony Thwaite leaning across and regarding me balefully once and saying, "Lay off the churchyards for a bit." And he was dead right.' To which Powell

---

[6]*From Parched Creek* (Bradford: Redbeck Press, 2001), p. 51.

[7]To their number we might add Jeremy Hooker, whose *Scattered Light* (London: Enitharmon Press, 2015) contains an 18-poem sequence entitled 'God's Houses', inspired by churches in England and Wales.

aptly responds, 'He didn't lay off them himself, though, did he?'[8] Thwaite has recently published a poem that reflects on this memory, acknowledging the plethora of church elegies and suggesting that 'an elegiac stance' has become commonplace. At the same time, he reiterates his sombre advice that the poet may be better off pursuing livelier themes:

> Shun the strewn bone-grounds, cemeteries and barrows,
> Keep out of churchyards, and avoid the grave:
> That ploughshare has pursued too many furrows,
> It knows too well how death-bed bards behave.[9]

Thwaite's recognition of the potential pitfalls facing the church elegist is a witty and spirited response to the melancholy and lugubrious tone of so many such poems.

Winnowing the possibilities down to the ninety or so church elegies that comprise this anthology has been an extraordinarily difficult task, and it was with great regret that I left many of them out. My central criterion in selecting was that the poem had to strike an elegiac note, a yearning for something lost; it need not explore the concept of belief, the practice of Christian worship, or an ethos of faith. (The survival of faith and worship in modern poetry is a worthy subject for another collection.) A second criterion was that a church must be the poem's literal focus, rather than merely a metaphor or a setting for meditation (as in Wordsworth's 'Tintern Abbey' or Eliot's 'Little Gidding'). A further criterion, but one that I have not entirely observed, is that the poem should focus on an Anglican parish church; because of the sheer irresistibility of some, I have included an occasional elegy about a Nonconformist chapel, a ruined medieval abbey or a Roman

---

[8]'Lessons in Survival', *PN Review* 37 (1984), p. 44.

[9]'A Word of Advice', *Going Out* (London: Enitharmon Press, 2015), p. 40.

Catholic shrine, as well as one or two on the institution and culture of the Church and its prayer book. The temptation to arrange the poems into neat thematic categories might have made for some fruitful comparisons; in the end, however, I decided against thematic groupings as that risked limiting the meanings and the interpretive possibilities of individual poems. Nevertheless, a number of recurring themes and motifs will become apparent as the reader makes his or her way through this collection.

The most common motif among church elegies is quite likely the church crawl. In the vein of Larkin's 'Church Going' and Betjeman's 'A Lincolnshire Church', the poet recounts a visit to a particular church and then explores the exterior and interior features of the church, perhaps with a Pevsner guide in hand. Take, for example, Charles Causley's visit to a Cornish church of thirteenth-century foundation:

I come, as fifty years ago,
Drawn by I know not what, to sound
A fabled shore, unlost, unfound,
Where in the shadow of the sun
Past, present, future, wait as one.

Contemplating the inevitable decay, the poet explores the personal and cultural consequences of the tidal flux of faith. With this motif, the personal experiences and mental discoveries seem to matter more than the particularities of the church itself.

In a closely related motif, the poet describes a living church from an omniscient perspective, rather than injecting himself or herself into the poem, as a church crawler. U.A. Fanthorpe imagines a sentient church in Essex, constructed in the Saxon era and still an active parish:

So old, it remembers
The people praying
Outside in the rain
Like football crowds.

Rather than the poet's personal encounter being the focus of meditation, such poems focus on the church building as a symbol of a sea change in faith and culture. Here, the church itself is vitally important, and the specificity of ecclesiastical detail compels the reader's attention.

A third motif focuses on particular features of church architecture and furnishing, such as bells, belfries, organs, stained glass, brass monuments, the reredos, the altar, rood screens and corbels. In one of Peter Scupham's poems, an ornamental devil has fallen to the ground:

Look in the grass; find his bolted feet
Still clawing for a toehold
On a flawed block of consecrated stone.

The image of the broken corbel reminds us of the fragility of faith and of the inevitable fragmentation of culture. Such poems also serve to remind us of the profound aesthetic beauty of the English parish church and of the historic artistry and skilled craftsmanship they reveal.

Many poets focus on the ruins of a church or abbey rather than on a living church; such poems tend to emphasize the decline of faith, a disruption in British culture or the historical importance of Christianity in Britain, and many of them look back to the Dissolution of the Monasteries and the fractured birth of the Church of England. Anthony Thwaite, for instance, describes what time has wrought from Henry VIII's destruction:

The hazed meadows of England grow over chancels
Where cattle hooves kick up heraldic tiles
And molehills heap their spoils above slumped walls.

The setting is beautiful but desolate, void of communal integrity and coherence. In poems about ruined churches and abbeys, the elegiac note may be most strongly felt.

A fifth motif can be found in poems with churchyard settings; such poems tend naturally to meditate on death and/or resurrection. Revisiting an ancestral burying ground, John Heath-Stubbs beseeches the churchyard itself to

> Carry these lives, these parts of lives, these yellow leaves
> Drifted in autumn from the tree of the world,
> On tides of intercession, down
> To a sea thirsty with love ...

Thus the poet imagines a culture united not just by the common fate of death but within a common faith. These poems may recall an older tradition of English verse, exemplified in the eighteenth-century graveyard poets and Gray's 'Elegy Written in a Country Churchyard'.

A final motif is the ecclesial landscape: poems that describe a landscape with a church at its heart or that suggest the church is the visible and imaginative centre of the English landscape. Elizabeth Jennings locates the beauty of England in its historic parish churches:

> Here all good that's England
> speaks in green flows of light, in church-bells ringing
> while afternoons are stretching out their arms ...

The historic church in its setting of natural simplicity creates an invitation to the alienated present to embrace the coherence of the past. Such poems respond to a tradition of semi-mythological English landscape poetry rooted in a pastoral yearning for an imagined golden age; one thinks perhaps of John of Gaunt's paean to England: 'This other Eden, demi-paradise'.

In essence, the poets of post-war Anglicanism embrace an idea that William Blake may very well have had in mind more than two hundred years ago, an idea revolutionized in the 1920s after Sir Hubert Parry set 'Jerusalem' to music and it became a beloved populist anthem. With its familiar closing line, 'Till we have built Jerusalem / In England's green and pleasant land', and its vaguely religious and imperial message, 'Jerusalem' occupies an unlikely position in English music in its broad and vital appeal to a people to whom notions of both empire and established Church are essentially dead or meaningless. Speaking within the context of Blake and Parry's anthem, Anglican bishop and theologian N.T. Wright has argued that 'Jerusalem was the place where heaven and earth came together, not in order to entice the inhabitants of earth away to a distant heaven, but in order to heal and enhance, to judge and to save, the present world.'[10] Poets who engage in this recuperation of Anglican memory are, I would argue, accepting the charge of spiritual empire-building in Blake and Parry's great anthem: they are building Jerusalem in England. Indeed, poet Tony Connor has used this metaphor to suggest that the poetic impulse is inherently religious though not orthodox: 'the poems that you write are the New Jerusalem, in the way that you ought to be living in the world.'[11] For poets of church elegies, Jerusalem is no mere site of collective spiritual memory but a living and transformative vision – a sense and a hope that the present world of chaos and fragmentation might be transmuted into identity, order and meaning.

---

[10]'Where Shall Wisdom Be Found?', Sermon at Durham Cathedral, 23 June 2007, www.ntwrightpage.com/sermons/Durham_Wisdom.htm, accessed 27 January 2015.

[11]'Tony Connor in Conversation with Tim Cumming and David Crystal, September 1986', *Slightly Soiled*, December 1986, p. 14.

FLEUR ADCOCK

At Great Hampden

That can't be it –
not with cherubs.
After all, they were Puritans.

All the ones on the walls are too late –
too curlicued, ornate, rococo –
17th century at least.

Well, then, says the vicar,
it will be under the carpets:
a brass.

He strips off his surplice,
then his cassock,
hardly ruffling his white hair.

He rolls the strip of red carpet;
I roll the underfelt.
It sheds fluff.

A brass with figures appears. Not them.
Another. Not them.
We've begun at the wrong end.

Room for one more? Yes.
There, just in front of the altar,
a chaste plaque and a chaste coat of arms.

It says what the book says:
'Here lieth the body of Griffith Hampden ...
and of Ann ...' No need to write it down.

Now we begin again, the vicar and I,
rolling the carpet back,
our heads bent to the ritual;

tweaking and tidying the heavy edges
we move our arms in reciprocal gestures
like women folding sheets in a launderette.

A button flips off someone's jacket.
Yours? I offer it to the vicar.
No, yours. He hands it back with a bow.

FLEUR ADCOCK

Kilpeck

We are dried and brittle this morning,
fragile with continence, quiet.
You have brought me to see a church.
I stare at a Norman arch in red sandstone
carved like a Mayan temple-gate;
at serpents writhing up the doorposts
and squat saints with South-American features
who stare back over our heads
from a panel of beasts and fishes.
The gargoyles jutting from under the eaves
are the colour of newborn children.

Last night you asked me
if poetry was the most important thing.

We walk on around the building
craning our heads back to look up
at lions, griffins, fat-faced bears.
The Victorians broke some of these figures
as being too obscene for a church;
but they missed the Whore of Kilpeck.
She leans out under the roof
holding her pink stony cleft agape
with her ancient little hands.
There was always witchcraft here, you say.

The sheep-track up to the fragments
of castle-wall is fringed with bright bushes.
We clamber awkwardly, separate.
Hawthorn and dog-rose offer hips and haws,
orange and crimson capsules, pretending
harvest. I taste a blackberry.
The soil here is coloured like brick-dust,
like the warm sandstone. A fruitful county.
We regard it uneasily.

There is little left to say
after all the talk we had last night
instead of going to bed –
fearful for our originality,
avoiding the sweet obvious act
as if it were the only kind of indulgence.

Silly perhaps.
We have our reward.
We are languorous now, heavy
with whatever we were conserving,
carrying each a delicate burden
of choices made or about to be made.
Words whisper hopefully in our heads.

Slithering down the track we hold hands
to keep a necessary balance.
The gargoyles extend their feral faces,
rosy, less lined than ours.
We are wearing out our identities.

SIMON ARMITAGE

Harmonium

The Farrand Chapelette was gathering dust
in the shadowy porch of Marsden Church.
And was due to be bundled off to the skip.
Or was mine, for a song, if I wanted it.

Sunlight, through stained glass, which on bright days
might beatify saints and raise the dead,
had aged the harmonium's softwood case
and yellowed the fingernails of its keys.
And one of its notes had lost its tongue,
and holes were worn in both the treadles
where the organist's feet, in grey, woollen socks
and leather-soled shoes, had pedalled and pedalled.

But its hummed harmonics still struck a chord:
for a hundred years that organ had stood
by the choristers' stalls, where father and son,
each in their time, had opened their throats
and gilded finches – like high notes – had streamed out.

Through his own blue cloud of tobacco smog,
with smoker's fingers and dottled thumbs,
he comes to help me cart it away.
And we carry it flat, laid on its back.
And he, being him, can't help but say
that the next box I'll shoulder through this nave

will bear the freight of his own dead weight.
And I, being me, then mouth in reply
some shallow or sorry phrase or word
too starved of breath to make itself heard.

PETER ARMSTRONG

Rains

Every blackened chapel yields its chiselled praises:
    harvest of the redbrick missions,
    flints of worship, faint incisions
in the faultless basalt face

of a theology. The faith retains
    a footing in the thin earth
    of hilltowns, brings forth
the blunt masonry of creeds among rains

that slant across our knowledge.
    And over the grass on blank slopes
    dry walls of dogma step
towards the millstone tops, the ridges

whose off-cast screes rain down
    shivered flints like an offering
    refused. Above, unseen birds sing
and the ravellings of cloud are undone.

CLIFF ASHBY

Fountains Abbey

We start as all the popular programmes start
With the commercials at the gate, the picture postcards,
Presents, films, the omnipresent lolly
Clutters up our history with our past.
In natural sequence to the world of commerce,
Authority demands its twentieth of a poem
To let the inheritors view their heritage.
All formal rites performed we now are free – to enter
And wander down to where a restless river
Fails to bear all our sins away.
There in the soft green meadow, mellow in the sun,
Stone upon prayer upon torn finger nail feels for the heavens
And crumbles in its own inadequacy.
My daughter asks, how many men have died
Creating this high monument to pride?
God knows! If all the men who died in its defence,
Were laid – with proper reverence – side by side
Within its longest shadow, this shallow valley
Would be levelled to its highest hill.
And still they come the concubines of truth.
The machinist, standing on the Abbot's tomb,
Baring her teeth into the camera's eye,
Has poised stiletto heels above his heart,
And in the infected blood the world may see
The adumbration of its history.

JULIET AYKROYD

The Angels of Muchelney

They visited the abbey late in the day.
Crosswinds
bully the dykewater,
rough up small trees. Queasily

the car heaves three old persons out.
They peer through gloom
at ruined walls,
foundations laid down *in principio*.

They see the beavered mason far ago
unroll the plans:
the abbot's hand:
hic capellam aedificio.

Wind goes for three old woolly hats,
flies whitefire hair.
Leaves run snickering.
Three vessels crab uneasily

together up the churchyard path,
sticks tremolo
at buttresses and pinnacles,
a gargoyle, yews. One lifts the latch.

Inside, a hitch: too dark to see.
Another says: Let's sit
in these tall pews
and wait. The third one finds the switch.

Light spins the stone to gold,
the glass to indigo.
Saints gleam in oils.
Ecce puer in praesepio.

High above, the angels flash
their tawny breasts.
In ice-cold air
white lilies float erratically.

The verger bustles in: Just thought she'd check.
You'll note the missing chancel tile (glares she).
Vandals hacked it out, would you believe.
A rare and ancient thing it was, coloured
ochre and vermilion, marked with a beast:
thirteenth century without a doubt.
How do these people dare, on Christmas Eve?
We must go, they said, and shuffled out.

The day is over now.
Prongs shape the sky.
Look, one murmurs, there in those small trees
the wicked wind shaking the mistletoe.
So ancient. So rare.

GEORGE BARKER

At Thurgarton Church

To the memory of my father

At Thurgarton Church the sun
burns the winter clouds over
the gaunt Danish stone
and thatched reeds that cover
the barest chapel I know.

I could compare it with
the Norse longboats that bore
burning the body forth
in honour from the shore
of great fjords long ago.

The sky is red and cold
overhead, and three small
sturdy trees keep a hold
on the world and the stone wall
that encloses the dead below.

I enter and find I stand
in a great barn, bleak and bare.
Like ice the winter ghosts and
the white walls gleam and flare
and flame as the sun drops low.

And I see, then, that slowly
the December day has gone.
I stand in the silence, not wholly
believing I am alone.
Somehow I cannot go.

Then a small wind rose, and the trees
began to crackle and stir
and I watched the moon by degrees
ascend in the window till her
light cut a wing in the shadow.

I thought: the House of the Dead.
The dead moon inherits it.
And I seem in a sense to have died
as I rise from where I sit
and out into darkness go.

I know as I leave I shall pass
where Thurgarton's dead lie
at those old stones in the grass
under the cold moon's eye.
I see the old bones glow.

No, they do not sleep here
in the long holy night of
the serene soul, but keep here
a dark tenancy and the right of
rising up to go.

Here the owl and soul shriek with
the voice of the dead as they turn
on the polar spit and burn
without hope and seek with
out hope the holy home below.

Yet to them the mole and
mouse bring a wreath and a breath
of the flowering leaves of the soul, and
it is from the Tree of Death
the leaves of life grow.

The rain, the sometime summer
rain on a memory of roses
will fall lightly and come a-
mong them as it erases
summers so long ago.

And the voices of those
once so much loved will flitter
over the nettled rows
of graves, and the holly tree twitter
like friends they used to know.

And not far away the
icy and paralysed stream
has found it also, that day the
flesh became glass and a dream
with no where to go.

Haunting the December
fields their bitter lives
entreat us to remember
the lost spirit that grieves
over these fields like a scarecrow.

That grieves over all it ever
did and all, all not
done, that grieves over
its crosspurposed lot:
to know and not to know.

The masterless dog sits
outside the church door
with dereliction haunting its
heart that hankers for
the hand that it loved so.

Not in a small grave
outside the stone wall
will the love that it gave
ever be returned, not for all
time or tracks in the snow.

More mourned the death of the dog
than our bones ever shall
receive from the hand of god
this bone again, or all
that high hand could bestow.

As I stand by the porch
I believe that no one has heard
here in Thurgarton Church
a single veritable word
save the unspoken No.

The godfathered negative
that responds to our mistaken
incredulous and heartbroken
desire above all to live
as though things were not so.

Desire to live as though the
two-footed clay stood up
proud never to know the
tempests that rage in the cup
under a rainbow.

Desire above all to live
as though the soul was stone,
believing we cannot give
or love since we are alone
and always will be so.

That heartbroken desire
to live as though no light
ever set the seas on fire
and no sun burned at night
or Mercy walked to and fro.

The proud flesh cries: I am not
caught up in the great cloud
of my unknowing. But that
proud flesh has endowed
us with the cloud we know.

To this the unspoken No
of the dead god responds
and then the whirlwinds blow
over all things and beyond
and the dead mop and mow.

And there in the livid dust
and bones of death we search
until we find as we must
outside Thurgarton Church
only wild grasses blow.

I hear the old bone in me cry
and the dying spirit call:
I have forfeited all
and once and for all must die
and this is all that I know.

For now in a wild way we
know that Justice is served
and that we die in the clay we
dread, desired, and deserved,
awaiting no Judgement Day.

JOHN BETJEMAN

A Lincolnshire Church

Greyly tremendous the thunder
Hung over the width of the wold
But here the green marsh was alight
In a huge cloud cavern of gold,
And there, on a gentle eminence,
Topping some ash trees, a tower
Silver and brown in the sunlight,
Worn by sea-wind and shower,
Lincolnshire Middle Pointed.
And around it, turning their backs,
The usual sprinkle of villas;
The usual woman in slacks,
Cigarette in her mouth,
Regretting Americans, stands
As a wireless croons in the kitchen
Manicuring her hands.
Dear old, bloody old England
Of telegraph poles and tin,
Seemingly so indifferent
And with so little soul to win.
What sort of church, I wonder?
The path is a grassy mat,
And grass is drowning the headstones
Sloping this way and that.
'Cathedral Glass' in the windows,
A roof of unsuitable slate –

Restored with a vengeance, for certain,
About eighteen-eighty-eight.
The door swung easily open
(Unlocked, for these parts, is odd)
And there on the South aisle altar
Is the tabernacle of God.
There where the white light flickers
By the white and silver veil,
A wafer dipped in a wine-drop
Is the Presence the angels hail,
Is God who created the Heavens
And the wide green marsh as well
Who sings in the sky with the skylark
Who calls in the evening bell,
Is God who prepared His coming
With fruit of the earth for his food
With stone for building His churches
And trees for making His rood.
There where the white light flickers,
Our Creator is with us yet,
To be worshipped by you and the woman
Of the slacks and the cigarette.

* * * * *

The great door shuts, and lessens
That roar of churchyard trees
And the Presence of God Incarnate
Has brought me to my knees.
'I acknowledge my transgressions'
The well-known phrases rolled
With thunder sailing over

From the heavily clouded wold.
'And my sin is ever before me.'
There in the lighted East
He stood in that lowering sunlight,
An Indian Christian priest.
And why he was here in Lincolnshire
I neither asked nor knew,
Nor whether his flock was many
Nor whether his flock was few
I thought of the heaving waters
That bore him from sun glare harsh
Of some Indian Anglican Mission
To this green enormous marsh.
There where the white light flickers,
Here, as the rains descend,
The same mysterious Godhead
Is welcoming His friend.

JOHN BETJEMAN

St Saviour's, Aberdeen Park, Highbury, London, N.

With oh such peculiar branching and over-reaching of wire
     Trolley-bus standards pick their threads from the London sky
Diminishing up the perspective, Highbury-bound retire
     Threads and buses and standards with plane trees volleying by
And, more peculiar still, that ever-increasing spire
     Bulges over the housetops, polychromatic and high.

Stop the trolley-bus, stop! And here, where the roads unite
     Of weariest worn-out London – no cigarettes, no beer,
No repairs undertaken, nothing in stock – alight;
     For over the waste of willow-herb, look at her, sailing clear,
A great Victorian church, tall, unbroken and bright
     In a sun that's setting in Willesden and saturating us here.

These were the streets my parents knew when they loved and won –
     The brougham that crunched the gravel, the laurel-girt paths
          that wind,
Geranium-beds for the lawn, Venetian blinds for the sun,
     A separate tradesman's entrance, straw in the mews behind,
Just in the four-mile radius where hackney carriages run,
     Solid Italianate houses for the solid commercial mind.

These were the streets they knew; and I, by descent, belong
    To these tall neglected houses divided into flats.
Only the church remains, where carriages used to throng
    And my mother stepped out in flounces and my father stepped
        out in spats
To shadowy stained-glass matins or gas-lit evensong
    And back in a country quiet with doffing of chimney hats.

Great red church of my parents, cruciform crossing they knew –
    Over these same encaustics they and their parents trod
Round through a red-brick transept for a once familiar pew
    Where the organ set them singing and the sermon let them
        nod
And up this coloured brickwork the same long shadows grew
    As these in the stencilled chancel where I kneel in the presence
        of God.

Wonder beyond Time's wonders, that Bread so white and small
    Veiled in golden curtains, too mighty for men to see,
Is the power which sends the shadows up this polychrome wall,
    Is God who created the present, the chain-smoking millions
        and me;
Beyond the throb of the engines is the throbbing heart of all –
    Christ, at this Highbury altar, I offer myself to Thee.

JOHN BETJEMAN

Sunday Morning, King's Cambridge

File into yellow candle light, fair choristers of King's
  Lost in the shadowy silence of canopied Renaissance stalls
In blazing glass above the dark glow skies and thrones and wings
  Blue, ruby, gold and green between the whiteness of the walls
And with what rich precision the stonework soars and springs
  To fountain out a spreading vault – a shower that never falls.

The white of windy Cambridge courts, the cobbles brown and dry,
  The gold of plaster Gothic with ivy overgrown,
The apple-red, the silver fronts, the wide green flats and high,
  The yellowing elm-trees circled out on islands of their own –
Oh, here behold all colours change that catch the flying sky
  To waves of pearly light that heave along the shafted stone.

In far East Anglian churches, the clasped hands lying long
  Recumbent on sepulchral slabs or effigied in brass
Buttress with prayer this vaulted roof so white and light and strong
  And countless congregations as the generations pass
Join choir and great crowned organ case, in centuries of song
  To praise Eternity contained in Time and coloured glass.

JOHN BETJEMAN

Uffington

Tonight we feel the muffled peal
    Hang on the village like a pall;
It overwhelms the towering elms –
    That death-reminding dying fall;
The very sky no longer high
    Comes down within the reach of all.
Imprisoned in a cage of sound
Even the trivial seems profound.

CHARLES CAUSLEY

At St Hilary

Between two Cornish seas, the spire
Blazes the land, the waving air.

The dark stem of a Celtic cross
Sprouts, half-grown, from the shallow grass.

A tomb, exploded, shows the bones
Of a young sycamore. Slant stones

Cram the graveyard like ships stormbound.
A wasted urn drips shard and sand.

Like auguries, two seabirds lie
Motionless in the squalling sky.

Through rain and wind and risen snow
I come, as fifty years ago,

Drawn by I know not what, to sound
A fabled shore, unlost, unfound,

Where in the shadow of the sun
Past, present, future, wait as one.

Only the breathing ash speaks true.
Nothing is new. Nothing is new

As the sea slinks to where I stand
Between the water and the land.

CHARLES CAUSLEY

St Protus & St Hyacinth, Blisland

The church, a stack of granite harvested
From Bodmin Moor, glints through uncovered trees
Above a valley loud with water, rocks,
Voices of bald-faced rooks that lurk and strut
High shelves of ash and sycamore. Beside

The porch the tilted ground is lit
With primrose, sharp-eyed daisy, daffodil.
The castor-oil plant gleams within a frame
Of window-stone, pure Georgian glass. Inside,
Along the nave, rough trunks of granite lean

Time-pressed this way, that way, in greying light.
Christ dies a gold death on the painted screen.
The altar glitters like a carousel.
The gilt tears of the Maries shine and fall.
Outside, a sudden pagan breeze, snow cool,

Flows from the waste of quoits and circled stones,
Roughens the grass skin of the goose-green where
Children shrill on the gibbet of a swing.
A boy in studded shirt and helmet revs
His bike up, circles endlessly the green

As though, for him, the day will never end.
Dark! Dark! the rooks warn. *Soon it will be dark!*
Unseen, an aircraft breaks the Cornish sky.
The two saints shudder on their granite plinth.
Pray for us, says Protus, says Hyacinth.

GLEN CAVALIERO

Fenland Churches

Are they floating,
or beached, like arks?
From each squat hill
they've spilled their freight
on the black fields –
toy pigs and sheds
and men in homes
like money-boxes, playthings for
the casual lubberly marsh wind.

Earth settling
on the fallow dead
pulls at a depressed
transept buttress
with a soft bubbling.
The belled tower
is ignored now;
children scribble in the visitor's book,
giggling, and the sanctuary lamp's extinct.

Sun rising
through farm doors
on pails of swill
silvers the pylons,
while the early birds
are broadcast, scanty

on scarce trees:
sound threads on silent wire
above each piping marble skull.

Everything's moving:
seagulls froth
in the tractor's wake,
and steeples twirl
their weathercocks
and surely sail
from tree to tree
as the farmer, bent on his own business,
hurries to market in the family brake.

Dutifully the waters
drain the soil.
Thunder withdraws;
the emptied clouds
are bland as oil
over the siloes
and the sugar beet.
Visitors under the neglected beacon
behold the rainbow's arch complete.

GLEN CAVALIERO

A Redundant Church

The dark has been expelled.
Thorns nuzzle under crumbled plaster
where the rood pales to a dust that volleys
on a flare of wings

signalling the order of release.
To stop and enter is to step right out
into more space than time contains
or quiet can sing.

GILLIAN CLARKE

Top Church

St Augustine's, Penarth

The prow of a smoky ship,
it sails down-channel currents
to the open sea;

souls' and sailors' guide, gnomon,
figurehead, riding the skyline
in a stream of light

on the summit of the climbing town
where I was a child,
and rain runs on the slant,

chutes of silver
sliding to sea and dock,
shops and streets and home,

it breasts the cloud,
a stony profile preaching continuity
in the face of turning tides.

JACK CLEMO

In Roche Church

Inland now, though soon to tread sea-sand again,
We kneel alone in the cool hill-top church,
Screened from Hensbarrow clay-smirch,
Guarded by clean pillars, free to marvel
At the way we ride the grey test, long past our vow.
Didn't the autumn winds howl warning
Of an ill-equipped and ill-timed venture in the wrong
Climate? Yet the calm tower
Is apt above our private gesture,
And the altar's mystery breathes through the centuries' dust
As her arm, eight years familiar, presses my waist.

There's a famous freak rock near us,
A black savage skull of a thing on the moor.
Monks built a chapel there and one wall stands
Facing the sea still, high on the schorl mass.
Gales from both coasts have struck the pinnacle
A thousand times, and shaken this church door
Which we approached under fragrant leafage
Up the lane from a July-scorched stile …
Something remains impregnable, holds evidence
Without a technique of defence.

Nimble cliff-climb up the crumbling stone stairs,
That we find true safety when storm knocks at night
Along our tissue of coast, swamping cave and landmark.

No: that's the cunning animal dodge,
Not for monks or the deeply married.
We must show man's stature, massive as the floundering assault;
We must cease to sharpen our wits
In training for trivial exits.

Man's way – our way at least – is a faith transcendent,
Hammered by storms from birth, clumsily sculptured,
Often seeming an obtuse image,
Neither skilled nor frantic when the boat splits
Or the tide traps, yet always preserved.
Nobody knows how. We are too intent
On the unseen touch, angel's wing, communion with a soul-mate,
To care whether our rescued feet
Tread sand or rock or moorland spur
Or the paved church. A random whim
Of unforced reverence has made us kneel,
Heads bowed, awed by our love's survival.

ANNE CLUYSENAAR

About the Church

Circled about the church, horsechestnuts hang cool
in their own shade, and at noon the steps
pearl with moisture. Tablets of stone,
askew and upright, weather even here

on their windward side: the names are effaced
haphazardly, as angles and paths determine.
Soon Brownies will befriend it. For now,
the churchyard teems with more natural neglect.

Still in flower, the loosestrife has long pods
unravelling cotton-white to a spray of seeds.
Twisting, a diseased sapling grows muscular.
This year's slabs lie grassy among the monuments.

Few have bouquets, even in their first September,
though most names here take living shapes
in the shops and offices, on the hill farms.
Such a place is a cut across fibres

of continuous time. Follow any one
tombstone, it will lead through ancestral crowds
into millions – beyond civilised man, and Man,
to wordless creatures, down to the persistent

minute beings whose efforts created us.
Vegetation, too, has its ancient history,
its unchronicled struggles, its baffled instincts.
The broken fibres are bleeding a memorial mould.

Craneflies and midges, in the filtered light,
make a brilliant, zigzag dust. Of this parish
now, I wonder how far back the dead
might recognise their only lives in mine.

TONY CONNOR

St Mark's, Cheetham Hill

Designed to dominate the district –
God being nothing if not large
and stern, melancholic from man's fall
(like Victoria widowed early) –
the church, its yard, were raised on a plateau
six feet above the surrounding green.
There weren't many houses then; Manchester
was a good walk away. I've seen
faded photographs: the church standing
amid strolling gentry, as though
ready to sail for the Empire's farthest parts –
the Union Jack at the tower's masthead
enough to quell upstart foreigners and natives.
But those were the early days. The city
began to gollop profits, burst
outward on all sides. Soon,
miles of the cheapest brick swaddled landmarks –
the church one. Chimes, that had used to wake
workers in Whitefield, died in near streets.

From our house (a part of the parish)
St Mark's is a turn right, a turn left,
and straight down Coke Street past the 'Horseshoe'.
The raised graveyard – full these many years –
overlooks the junction of five streets:
pollarded plane trees round its edge,

the railings gone to help fight Hitler.
Adam Murray of New Galloway
'who much improved the spinning mule'
needs but a step from his tomb to peer in
at somebody's glittering television.
Harriet Pratt, 'a native of Derby',
might sate her judgement-hunger with chips
were she to rise and walk twenty yards.
The houses are that close. The church,
begrimed, an ugly irregular box
squatting above those who once filled it
with faith and praise, looks smaller now
than in those old pictures. Subdued
by a raincoat factory's bulk, the Kosher
Slaughter House next door, its dignity
is rare weddings, the Co-op hearse,
and hired cars full of elderly mourners.

The congregations are tiny these days,
few folk could tell you whether it's 'High' or 'Low'.
The vicar's name, the times of services,
is specialized knowledge. And fear has gone:
the damp, psalmed, God of my childhood has gone.
Perhaps a boy delivering papers
in winter darkness before the birds awake,
keeps to Chapel Street's far side, for fear
some corpse interred at his ankle's depth
might shove a hand through the crumbling wall
and grab him in passing; but not for fear
of black religion – the blurred bulk
of God in drizzle and dirty mist,

or hooded with snow on his white throne
watching the sparrow fall.
                              Now, the graveyard –
its elegant wrought-ironwork wrenched,
carted away; its rhymed epitaphs,
urns of stone and ingenious scrolls
chipped, tumbled, masked by weeds –
is used as a playground. Shouting children
Tiggy between the tombs.
                              On Saturdays
I walk there sometimes – through the drift
of jazz from open doors, the tide
of frying fish, and the groups of women
gossiping on their brushes – to see the church,
its God decamped, or dead, or daft
to all but the shrill hosannas of children
whose prayers are laughter, playing such parts
in rowdy games, you'd think it built
for no greater purpose, think its past
one long term of imprisonment.

Little survives Authority's cant
but the forgotten, the written-off,
and the misunderstood. The Methodist chapel's
been bought by the Jews for a synagogue;
Ukrainian Catholics have the Wesleyan's
sturdy structure built to outlast Rome –
and men of the district say St Mark's
is part of a clearance area. Soon
it will be down as low as rubble
from every house that squeezed it round,

to bed a motorway and a new estate.
Or worse: repainted, pointed, primmed –
as becomes a unit in town-planners'
clever dreams of a healthy community –
will prosper in dignity and difference,
the gardened centre of new horizons.

Rather than this I'd see a ruin,
and picture the final splendours of decay:
Opposing gangs in wild 'Relievo',
rushing down aisles and dusty pews
at which the houses look straight in
past broken wall; and late-night drunkards
stumbling their usual short-cut home
across uneven eulogies, fumbling
difficult flies to pour discomfort out
in comfortable shadows, in a nave
they praise with founts, and moonlit blooms of steam.

IAIN CRICHTON SMITH

In Luss Churchyard

Light strikes the stone bible like a gong:
blank leaves gape open. Greenness of grass is most
what, raging round the slabs, astonishes
the casual visitor drifting like a ghost
among the inscriptions and the wishes
chiselled on stone, prayed for a dead tongue.

A bird flickers from bough to windless bough
unsettled, frenzied perhaps with heat
or violence of the breast, a pagan joy.
The stranger remarks anew his moving feet
so constantly labouring in his employ
and walking without thought as they do now:

and the very inscriptions mirror modes of death –
the early stately and the later terse
(the very early almost invisible).
Consider how this eighteenth-century verse
glides with a quiet charm through pastoral
landscapes of the wandering breath.

Here however a skull, there crossed bones
leap out with tigerish instancy, like fire
burning through paper: with a savage force
punch through electric noon where the hands perspire

and prickle with the sun. This is indeed a coarse
imagery to be carved on harmless stones.

The adjacent river rambles quietly on
with wayward music, hardly disturbing even
the image of a leaf or stone or stick
but holding all the amplitude of heaven –
the fiery blueness of a composed Atlantic –
arching an earth poised in the breathless noon

where living and dead turn on the one hinge
of a noon intensely white, intensely clear.
The eyes read dates: the hands steady and rest
on leaning stone without a twitch of fear
merely an aimless curiosity. The breast,
empty with indifference, broods in change.

Yet, should a charge populous, terrible,
burst through the feeding greenness, capsizing this
mound like a knotted table, knees would sink
into the imponderable abyss
where the one star burns with a convulsive wink
in a white sky, blown outwards like a bubble.

The silence holds. A saw nags at a tree.
The settled bird chirps briefly while a breeze
ruffles its breast. The eye confused by dates
is pleasurably excited by the trees
arching a coolness over the heavy gates.
Therefore out of the noon's implacable sea

of hammered light the feet, still steady, go.
The hands touch wood and push the gate away
from the dreaming body which casts a little shade.
Out of the hectic greenness into a day
of dusty roadways the feet, suddenly gripping, wade
gathering power, changing to swift from slow.

KEVIN CROSSLEY-HOLLAND

Angels at St Mary's

'The angels have gone.'
Church Guide, Walsham-le-Willows

Up among bleached stars and suns
Are the tongues, protruding, oak pegs
Wanting their smiling high-fliers.

The fledglings heard black hints
And saw battle-lights advancing.
They conferred, they spread their wings.

Or did they become spirits of
Themselves? Angels rearranged,
Acute angles where clear sound and

Sunlight cross? They are in the air.

The angel terminals in the lovely oak roof have disappeared. There is a strong tradition in the village that they were taken into safekeeping during the Reformation, and one wing was still to be seen at the Vicarage (now the Old Vicarage) in the 1870s [KC-H].

KEVIN CROSSLEY-HOLLAND

In Latter Days

After two or three
had gathered in His name,

the purring began.
Showers of bright semi-quavers
and the mountains skipped,
floods clapped their hands.

In the great emptiness,
on your knee-bones,
you dreamed about decay
and holy mildew
all over chiming England.

Again we sang;
then an officer trundled up
to the savage lectern
with his babyfood bible.

O ye gods …

Divine authority,
our fathers' cadences,
and their fathers' fathers,
shuffled off.

Committee-speak!
The work of the worthy
with flat feet,
fearful of fire and unknowing.

In the terrible gloom
you lowered your head,
accomplice
while the Word
was betrayed by the word.

SIMON CURTIS

Leaving Towcester Vicarage

Up and down the stairs, with clump of boot on board,
  The Pickfords men moved items, one by one;
    We talked of football with them over tea –
  The Hesketh bike, and what the Council'd done
    About its car-park scheme – phlegmatically,
      As if nothing untoward;
Sat round the table this time, though, we knew
  Beyond the door there, in the stone-flagged hall,
  The books had gone, no Cruikshank on the wall …
The Cobblers start next season up at Crewe.

Keep busy now, and don't give in to gloom;
  I take my matches out, and then crouch down
    To set alight the mildewed leather box
Of juvenilia I've dumped on the brown
    Dry earth, where iceberg roses and mauve phlox,
      Serene as ever, bloom.
Then the acrid blue smoke-ribbons rise;
  While cool Madonna lilies in their row
  Next to the limestone wall, as ever, glow,
A past's detritus disperses to the skies.

The town-hall chimes, the church bell just behind,
  The 'synagogue' you won't lock any more.
    Its tolls, its quarter-peals, the eight o'clock,
  And big Vic Burt who rang them, strict as law,

Blacksmith and verger, gone. How much comes back,
    Bewildering, to mind!
Old Cyril Buckland's hand-cranked roundabout
    One damp June garden fete I helped to run;
    His wedding, with white horses and a brougham!
Like me, he's balding now, and getting stout.

Foxed pages of old registers recall
    The seventeenth century names we know –
        Dunkley, Loveridge, Allen and Linnell,
Father to son to son, unfolding slow
    Succession in the town, soul after soul,
        Each individual;
The parsons' scripts mark, birth by birth, each name,
    Yet telescoped as in a wink of time;
    Revs Lockwood, Roper, Ford, now you. That chime's
Rung out each day, three centuries, the same.

How we would listen to Mum's Delius,
    Together on the drawing-room settee,
        Two teenaged boarding schoolboys there, all ears!
Like yesterday, it all comes back to me,
    Though you've not sat to play in recent years –
        That's what arthritis does.
And beds undug, well, what's the point, you say,
    We're off, we've grubbed up roots and bulbs to take
    For the 'box' we've bought – then, quietly, make
Your joke, it's a box we end up in, anyway.

Things helped to mar the last few months we had;
    Those plans to sell the house – *as offices!*

They thought, the Goths, they'd get a new one built;
And sited in the garden, if you please!
    That Canon Urquhart in it to the hilt;
      A stinker, and quite mad.
The PCC, thank goodness, threw it out –
    The church is stuffed with bland committee men,
    Who'd join the Baptists, outlaw Series One;
None of them's an earthly what it's all about.

And one last time I wander round the side
    Along the passage we shot airguns in
      To have a pee (old force of habit still)
By outhouse fete flags, folding chairs, the bin,
    Then leave, no looking back, by strength of will
      To shrug off what has died.
And pegs still on the line – so normal, all –
    Under the beech whose grape-dark August leaf
    Lent relish to the heart yet, crossed by grief;
Short tenancy of richness; leaves must fall.

I called in at Cold Higham afterward,
    Where my nephew and my niece were staying,
      She engrossed in *The Boy Friend*'s film remake
He with a frisbee in the garden playing.
    We spoke of school, swapped jokes, I tried to shake
      Dismay off – word by word.
I'll not scythe nettles down again below
    The apple-tree tangle, or feast my eye
    On our yew and copper-beech. And so, good-bye.
Soon on that bonfire ash, new grass will grow.

DONALD DAVIE

The Priory of St Saviour, Glendalough

A carving on the jamb of an embrasure,
'Two birds affronted with a human head
Between their beaks' is said to be
'Uncertain in its significance but
A widely known design.' I'm not surprised.

For the guidebook cheats: the green road it advises
In fact misled; and a ring of trees
Screened in the end the level knoll on which
St Saviour's, like a ruin on a raft,
Surged through the silence.

I burst through brambles, apprehensively
Crossed an enormous meadow. I was there.
Could holy ground be such a foreign place?
I climbed the wall, and shivered. There flew out
Two birds affronted by my human face.

C. DAY-LEWIS

Seen from the Train

Somewhere between Crewkerne
And Yeovil it was. On the left of the line
Just as the crinkled hills unroll
To the plain. A church on a small green knoll –
A limestone church,
And above the church
Cedar boughs stretched like hands that yearn
To protect or to bless. The whole

Stood up, antique and clear
As a cameo, from the vale. I swear
It was not a dream. Twice, thrice had I found it
Chancing to look as my train wheeled round it.
But this time I passed,
Though I gazed as I passed
All the way down the valley, that knoll was not there,
Nor the church, nor the trees it mounded.

What came between to unsight me? …
But suppose, only suppose there might be
A secret look in a landscape's eye
Following you as you hasten by,
And you have your chance –
Two or three chances
At most – to hold and interpret it rightly,
Or it is gone for aye.

There was a time when men
Would have called it a vision, said that sin
Had blinded me since to a heavenly fact.
Well, I have neither invoked nor faked
Any church in the air,
And little I care
Whether or no I shall see it again.
But blindly my heart is racked

When I think how, not twice or thrice,
But year after year in another's eyes
I have caught the look that I missed today
Of the church, the knoll, the cedars – a ray
Of the faith, too, they stood for,
The hope they were food for,
The love they prayed for, facts beyond price –
And turned my eyes away.

U.A. FANTHORPE

Greensted Church

Stone has a turn for speech.
Felled wood is silent
As mown grass at mid-day.

These sliced downright baulks
Still wear the scabbed bark
Of unconquered Epping
Though now they shore up
Stone, brick, glass, gutter
Instead of leaf or thrush.

Processing pilgrims,
The marvels that drew them –
Headless king, holy wolf –
Have all fined down to
Postcards, a guidebook,
Mattins on Sunday.

So old, it remembers
The people praying
Outside in the rain
Like football crowds. So old
Its priests flaunted tonsures
As if they were war-cries.

Odd, fugitive, like
A river's headwaters
Sliding a desultory
Course into history.

U.A. FANTHORPE

St James's, Charfield

(a redundant church)

Someone has left riddles here,
Relic of the interrogative mode
Licensed to be used in churches.

The seven signs of Charfield:

A *bier*, since all flesh is,
And churchyards are never redundant,
Dying remaining the most
Favoured single activity.

A *sparrow*, claws up, for the fallen,
And to remind us how many we are worth.

A *Bible*, revised but sinister:
He also suppressed the hill-shrines
And the sacred poles in Judah.
Jehoshaphat, professing urban religion.

An *organ*, midget, defunct,
Which roared *Aargh* like a maniac
Being touched.

Emptiness, left behind by pews,
Vestments, guidebooks, kneelers,
The gaudy clutter of mortality. What stays
Is anybody's guess. It flutters,
And is full of light.

Pinned to the door, a *list*
Of the churchyard's flora: *I do hope*
That you will be able to manage
This interesting site in the best way
For the wildlife. And names,
Instead of the flower-arrangers, the flowers:
Cow-parsley, columbine, cuckoo-pint, daisy.

Last, the *memorial*,
In discreet granite memory
Of *those who lost their lives*
In the railway accident at Charfield:
Persons from Belper, Milverton,
Gloucester, Sheffield; couples
From Leicester, Derby, Plymouth;
Two children, never identified,
The hairs of whose heads someone
Omitted to number.

                                        Please,
No weedkiller to be used in the churchyard.

U.A. FANTHORPE

'Soothing and Awful'

(Visitors' Book at Montacute Church)

You are meant to exclaim. The church
Expects it of you. Bedding plants
And polished brass anticipate a word.

Visitors jot a name,
A nationality, briskly enough,
But find *Remarks* beyond them.

I love English churches!
Says Friedrichshafen expansively.
The English are more backward. They come,

Certainly, from Spalding, Westbury-on-Trym,
The Isle of Wight; but all the words
They know are: *Very Lovely; Very Peaceful; Nice.*

A giggling gaggle from Torquay Grammar,
All pretending they can't spell *beautiful*, concoct
A private joke about the invisible organ.

A civilized voice from Cambridge
Especially noticed the well-kept churchyard.
Someone from Dudley, whose writing suggests tight shoes,

Reported *Nice and Cool*. The young entry
Yelp their staccato approval:
Super! Fantastic! Jesus Lives! Ace!

But what they found,
Whatever it was, it wasn't what
They say. In the beginning,

We know, the word, but not here,
Land of the perpetually-flowering cliché,
The rigid lip. Our fathers who piled

Stone upon stone, our mothers
Who stitched the hassocks, our cousins
Whose bones lie smooth, harmonious around –

However majestic their gifts, comely their living,
Their words would be thin like ours; they would join
In our inarticulate anthem: *Very Cosy.*

ROY FULLER

Youth Revisited

The hastening cloud grows thin; the sun's pale disc
Swells, haloes, then bursts out and warms the stone,
Pitching the yew's black tent on brilliant green.
A dozen years have gone since last I saw
This tiny church set on the parkland's edge
Between the glistening hunters and the cattle,
A Sunday exercise for week-end guests,
And I approach it conscious that emotion
Ought to be suffered, as indeed it is.
Did I live here and was I happy then?
A war more innocent, an age of man
Removed, my poems thick with formal doom
And baseless faith in humans. Years that now
Pass with the clarity of hours then
Record the degeneration of the nerves
And the world situation, make a golden
Time from that decade of infirm belief.

I am half glad to find the place has marked
Dramatically my absence. All the roof
Has gone, grass flutters on the broken stone,
A notice says *These walls are dangerous.*
Through unglazed windows marble monuments
Are glimpsed like modest spinsters in their baths.
Bombs or neglect, informants are not sure:
In any case the church will now decay

With other luxuries. The horses are
Not here, no doubt the mansion house beyond
The lake is requisitioned by the state,
And furrows creep across the pleasure ground.

I wonder if my son completely fails
To grasp my halting reconstruction of
My youth. Here, where we brought him in our arms
Was neat then, facing time with fortitude.
The statues in the gloom stood for their moral,
The wicked viscount's smoke rose from the house,
The evils of the epoch had not quite
Made rational the artist's accidie.

And yet, the clock moved on another twelve,
He would have something still to put to his son.
The jet planes slither overhead, a frog
Throbs in the dust half-way across the road,
Over two fields a saw scrapes like a bird.
Creatures, machines and men live yet among
The partial, touching ruins of their world.

ROGER GARFITT

Rites of Passage

to Tony Conran, in the year of his marriage,
the birth of his first child, and his father's death.

Comfortable words, framed
in darker times than ours,
are ruined archways,

rusted gates, lych gate
or kissing gate, beaten paths
to love or death

that dwindle out of use.
As our forefathers knew,
their ways are grass

– a by-way their sense of
comfortable, a castle stump
in the marches

that marks where a language
lost its fight. The formless
is given ground.

A name thumbed from the map
wears a way back to
the capital.

Death blues a nail, and
climbs the ring finger
to the heart.

We are raided by
the inarticulate. *Be sober,*
be vigilant,

the Apostle says – watchwords since
requisitioned by General Booth
and Captain Lynch

while *our adversary…*
as a roaring lion is
all but extinct.

The last enemy is
amnesia. The synapses
lapse in the mind,

the keystones fall to the grass.
Roadmenders are few, roadmakers
almost none. All

but lost to philology
the adjective's active
ability

to say *comfort* where there is
nothing to be said, at *Brig o' Dread*
to find foothold.

Or before this other, this
excellent mystery, to give good luck
at the threshold.

The language is at a loss:
uncomfortable, unaccustomed
and unversed.

'Now cool it!' – honeyed voices
over the rasp of Jeremiah
grinding his axe –

'Adam has transplanted the Garden.
Time is becoming habitable
for the first time.

Ask the dead. They'd be here tomorrow
with "*We should have your problems!*"'
And so they would.

They'd have the transplanted Garden
in one perpetual season,
stationary

in an arrested prime: every
floret held back to a *floruit*,
a moment's grace

or else … the disgrace,
the fade, the dissolve
into incoherence.

What would they say, the stone-
breaking dead, who broke the unspoken
into metal,

links of an embanked and culverted
spine, a strait road that stretched
to meet their god?

Death is the way we live. In time
the myth comes, and gathers us
to our long home.

Only ours is comfortless:
the consuming young; obsolescence
built-into the old.

Can we match our forefathers' active
speech, that *made* a good marriage
or a good death,

from the passive registry
the language has become, the syllables'
expanding files

of *developmental life crises*
or *maladaptive conflict
situations?*

While the elderly subscribe
to *Death Education*, a course in
creative dying.

Chequer of cells in the rock,
psychosis is all we keep
of the *psyche*,

the gauze of a butterfly.
All the more need, then,
to hold our ground

in the lyric, in the spring
of the steps we inherit
from the bull leap

at Knossos, somersault
as you have, who tumble
for Our Lady,

executing figure after figure
of speech for a scholar's
summa cum laude,

or finding words for the postman
who dies of a stroke, the local,
everyday loss.

Savant et jongleur, you are
living proof that art can
be generous,

a field full of folk where
the loquacious pay heed
to the tongue-tied

and serious play is the making
of us, the arch we thread through
to the cradle.

JOHN GREENING

A Huntingdonshire Elegy

Caught in the space between Christmas and New Year, idly
wondering about Huntingdonshire churches: who uses them now?
Are we even closer to the fulfilling of Larkin's prophecy?

When the man in the four-by-four attempted to winch off
the lightning conductor from Little Staughton spire for the copper,
was that the beginning of the final act? Iconoclasts move

beyond stained glass and altar screens: they strike
at Michelangelo's very finger and bring down the roof. We snub
the churches around us and they ignore us back; though, on my bike

before Christmas, I reached Little Gidding and found the chapel
unlocked: not a soul, the community gone, a page
of signatures and Eliot on the wall; a bell, no steeple –

nothing for thieves or lightning. But something as shocking
struck me as I put on my cycle clips again and rode
home to wrap up your present – that book by Richard Dawkins.

JOHN GREENING

A Huntingdonshire

Nocturne

They dance like paper cut-outs on a length of fishing line
across our windy county. The tail of a kite so high
it's almost out of sight, the cross of a man's agony

held by a child with his hands together on holy ground.
They dance – a tower, a spire; a porch, a flying buttress –
to the fantasia of an organ, to the thunder-repelling carillon

and they call to dance those who have forgotten what it means
to stop walking, stop running and skip, hop,
hornpipe to the music in the nave. If ever the wind drops,

what then? And already there is a change in the weather. One paper
cut-out is gone, another is torn, the kite itself is flying
erratically, the dance is uncertain, the music is played by old

arthritic fingers, there are bell-ropes hanging unused. Sing
your Shaker tunes, sing your Wesley anthems, sing, sing
hymns ancient and modern, for the child with his hands together,

for the children who will find the paper fragments littering the
    landscape,
make boats of them, make a treasure hunt of them, and not know
the secret in these crossed sticks, this fabric, the very wind.

GEOFFREY GRIGSON

West Window

Consolations were: Christ, Heaven,
Judgement, devils at the mouth
Of great Leviathan, glow of these
Through minds stained with the bright
Salts of cobalt, copper, iron. *And now –*
What now, whispers to himself upon
His knees the priest, *now time hurts me,*
Home walks away, and deserts me,
And everything is beast?

JOHN HEATH-STUBBS

Churchyard of Saint Mary Magdalene, Old Milton

Here, where my father lies under the ornamental plum,
Geese step in the next farm-field, while to the Rectory elms
The rooks fly home. *Dominus exaltatio mea* –
The eagle rising with its sprig of acorns.

Feet deep in sticky clay, under the kempt grasses,
Under the anglo-saxon, and the celtic crosses,
The Indian judges lie, the admirals, the solicitors,
The eccentric ladies, and the shopkeepers,
The unenterprising who would not go to the town,
The charwoman with a cleft palate, the jobbing gardener,
And the four Germans who fell, some years back,
Out of a sky of trouble, smashed
In an empty field – these have
Their regulation crosses too, of wood,
And scattered flowers, left by the prisoners:
The old woman whom I meet
Remarks that after all they were somebody's sons
And we would do as much for our people.

'The writer returns to the scene of his childhood' –
Where he loitered and looked at the rooks and the geese and
    the turkeys,

Or sought for wild barley by the churchyard gate –
The caterpillar-grass
Whose insect heads climb slowly up your sleeve;
The rootless writer, filling his own lungs
With a gust of country air. A grey afternoon,
And in the sky, the promise of evening rain.

Where people come to take the air and die,
Ending their lives here on an adequate pension,
A sickly child, brought there by careful parents,
Might mend in the salt breeze. From six to twenty-four
Home was this scattered residential village of bungalows,
Of gabled villas, and neglected fallows,
Crazy-paving, gravel, and tarmac. Now he comes back
And stands unrecognized among these graves.

The church here under John, that lackland king,
(The guide-book says), rebuilt under Elizabeth:
(The tower still stands, four-square, looks down upon
The village green, a row of shops, a garage
Crimson and yellow with petrol-pumps,
A line of cottages, a blacksmith's forge –
A child, I remember that darkness and smoke and music –
Two adjacent public-houses, the 'George' and 'Wheatsheaf',
And the post-office store, where stands behind the jumble
Of picture-postcards, cigarettes, and buttons,
The dusty case with its stuffed gannet and guillemot).
Rebuilt under Elizabeth, restored under Victoria,
(The green distempered walls, peeling to white patches,
Which look, at sermon time, the shapes of islands –
White islands, in a green smooth-glistening sea).

Lie here the serfs, the yeomen, and the gentry,
Under their mounds, and single stones, and vaults yellow with
    lichen;
Of all those faces, only one gazes still –
Queen Anne's colonel, in effigy, pompous his armour,
His helmet beside him, a ringleted wig of stone
Framing his vacant brow. His sword, that steel blade,
Which he drew against the French, is hung above him
Over the blurred inscription, on the left of the porch.

A torch borne in the wind, a drift of sparks and smoke
As the racer rounds the track in the bright sunlight,
Dust-puff, and dream, and shadow …

A drop of rain, a large, warm drop,
A rustle in the tresses of the elm,
A breath of perfume, twitched by the light breeze,
From the fading flowers laid on the Italian marble –
But these evoke the sudden splendour of bright hair
Unloosed from the darkness of a penitent snood,
Sweetness, and the splintering of the alabaster-sealed heart;
Somewhere among these tombs a woman's voice is sobbing;
Among these fragments grope the white and delicate hands
Of the Anointer of the Dead, who comes in the dark hour
Bringing her spices for the early dawn.

A fountain of lamentation above the firmament, a human
River of tears, that knows all streets, alleys, and dark courts,
And bears upon its little waves
Sticks and straws and draggled cigarette-ends,
The gutter's refuse and corruption, on

Past Roman causeways, through black hearts of cities.
A girl, mad as grief, trudging the hard roads;
A woman, with a few ripe ears, in a country of famine;
The august queen of the shrunken banks of Nile,
Who seeks the body of her murdered Lord;
A girl, sorry as sin, and broken as contrition.

Lady of Magdala's tower, and the dower of Bethany,
You who are called patron here, forgive
The little lives, partial and fugitive existences,
The gestures of love frozen in a pose of propriety,
And starved desire, with malice that lies on a turning bed;
Forgive the tyrannies of the hearthstone, and the small politics
Of the local interest, the lonely and the dull.
Ask pardon for the community without a heart, and the betrayal
Of the backward years and the uncomplaining dead.
Carry these lives, these parts of lives, these yellow leaves
Drifted in autumn from the tree of the world,
On tides of intercession, down
To a sea thirsty with love, where the breakers lift
White triumphing hands – insatiable;
And the free gull tacks to the courteous southern stars,
With arched and frost-pale pinion:
Oh, in Death's garden be
Prime witness of the only Resurrection.

MICHAEL HENRY

St Martin in the Field

It was a world of brown holland
of Miss Havishams and Estellas
until poverty was diverted
from the reading rooms of libraries –

an unofficial congregation sleeps out
full forty winks of prayer
touching reassurance in the oaken pews
remembering when life was new and Sunday-smelling –

secular sermons to 'Mind your wallet.
Do not leave unattended valuables ...'
the Church's treasure is a dish of sunlight
that streams in through the unstained glass –

there is that rustling noise of silence
shuffling conversation and newspapers
taking little liberties with God –
this is the pit shift

St Martin in the Field
field grey down the tunnel of a gun.

MICHAEL HENRY

Slipper Chapel

The lime-trees have a green chalk dust
like teacher's nicotine to touch;
there is a notice 'Beware of Adders'
like 'Cave Canem' as if the snakes were guard snakes –
we take off our slippers
and make pilgrimage in the ruined chapel:
clerestory choir corbel
the fragments are a glossary of terms –
from Hailes to Glastonbury
Tintern to Minster Lovell…
I dig under an upturned divot
exhume cathedral treasure
with ventricles of root and nestling peat –
the cold heart of our lady chapel.

GEOFFREY HILL

Epiphany at Saint Mary and All Saints

The wise men, vulnerable in ageing plaster,
are borne as gifts
to be set down among the other treasures
in their familial strangeness, mystery's toys.

Below the church the Stour slovens
through its narrow cut.
On service roads the lights cast amber salt
slatted with a thin rain doubling as snow.

Showings are not unknown: a six-winged seraph
somewhere impends – it is the geste of invention,
not the creative but the creator spirit.
The night air sings a colder spell to come.

GEOFFREY HILL

Loss and Gain

Pitched high above the shallows of the sea
lone bells in gritty belfries do not ring
but coil a far and inward echoing
out of the air that thrums. Enduringly,

fuchsia-hedges fend between cliff and sky;
brown stumps of headstones tamp into the ling
the ruined and the ruinously strong.
Platonic England grasps its tenantry

where wild-eyed poppies raddle tawny farms
and wild swans root in lily-clouded lakes.
Vulnerable to each other the twin forms

of sleep and waking touch the man who wakes
to sudden light, who thinks that this becalms
even the phantoms of untold mistakes.

BRIAN HINTON

All Saints

An angel folds its wings, huddled warm.
I pass by, cosy as the couples lying ended;
different dates, their joint lives ended
by a stonemason's chisel, 'greatly mourned'.

The boneyard ebbs down to the sea:
despite the yews, buds foretell the Spring.
Flowers die in jars, from death snowdrops spring,
gulls circle back like white débris.

I cloak in my warmth, feel its passing, but
walk towards the cold shore's culmination,
The church clock ticks towards culmination.
The lych gate swings sharply shut.

JEREMY HOOKER

St Cross

1

Over the footworn step,
between old walls
that have soaked in
river-damp, in
the twilight nave,

there is something
that is not ourselves.

Something to grasp
if we could name it;
like the tile
with its legend:
                    Have mynde

2

The damp, still dusk
of December breaks,

and light sweeps the aisle
slowly, bringing back
grey sky, grey stone:

St Cross
signing the valley
with a man's power
and his penitence,
mindful of
Henry of Winchester,
soldier-bishop,
turning from the world.

3

The light as it passes
reveals an old woman
kneeling at altar rails
of a side chapel.

No ghost, but one
completely given;
as if the body of stone
had formed round her,
and she would be here
after it has gone.

FRANCES HOROVITZ

Country Afternoon

we buy postcards
sepia-tinted
putting extra money, carefully, in the box

a lone tourist
made nervous by laughter
and the child climbing on tombstones
hurries towards the lych-gate
shuts it with an echoing click

a church noted by Betjeman
saddle-backed, herring-boned
tiny, cool
more ancient than its written history
a god's eye in Cotswold fields:
outside, the graven cross, six centuries worn
is a single shaft to heaven

from the crypt I look up
see your face for an instant
dark against sunlight
still as a stone knight

a wood-pigeon clatters –
from a smouldering bonfire
smoke wavers upwards

we gaze into the rectory orchard
heavy with forbidden fruit
dahlias in shocks lean towards us

across the lane
five geese from a fairy tale
cows gathered peaceably to be milked
a muddy ford with minnows
no sound or sight of other human

fifteen adults in this community
a few children and the old
where are they all –
indoors, or vanished long ago
into the hedgerows, the rolling fields?

at the edge of the wood a horse chases a cow

'an afternoon out of time,' you say
'fifty years or more ago
– if I built a church it would be like this'

I pick flowers that will not last the journey home

heat dances on tarmac
the child runs towards the car

where to go from here?

TED HUGHES

Heptonstall Old Church

A great bird landed here.

Its song drew men out of rock,
Living men out of bog and heather.

Its song put a light in the valleys
And harness on the long moors.

Its song brought a crystal from space
And set it in men's heads.

Then the bird died.

Its giant bones
Blackened and became a mystery.

The crystal in men's heads
Blackened and fell to pieces.

The valleys went out.
The moorland broke loose.

ELIZABETH JENNINGS

Somerset

Such gentle open slopes, such lack of drama.
A cottage there and there a tiny town
lodged in a valley, rivers overflowing
after four rainy months
but all is drying now as ubiquitous sun
points out a church spire then a gaze of windows
an almost temperate time but not quite yet.
Who knows what March may bring? Perhaps some snow
but for this Sunday late in February
Spring slips its head round corners of big clouds
and they are silvered by the raptured sun
and by me gazing. Here all good that's England
speaks in green flows of light, in church-bells ringing
while afternoons are stretching out their arms
before the good day of our clocks put forward.

P.J. KAVANAGH

Westwell Churchyard, Oxfordshire

Sky mother-of-pearl. Oyster-colour sun
A furry lemon,
Silent, full of silences.
Birdless windless trees hold breath;
Stream tinkles to pond to be frozen to death.
Silence: a hand clapped over a mouth;
Violent, with suppressed violences.
Earth is preoccupied, waiting to know
The soft grope of snow.
Muscles of a bough crack, pistol-shot, echo echo…
On a little mound
Near stream, by pond,
A church: a square of yellow stone,
Some of it ferried over seas from Caen
In boats too light, you would have thought,
To bear the weight,
Ages of faith ago.
Moss on the church-yard gate.
Green grass prickles the hoar-frost sheet.
And then the moment like a film-shot freezes.
Perceived, not seen, almost out of frame:
Joy. A presence,
Transforming all the other presences:

And leaning against your new-cut yellow stone
A splash of carmine
A scatter of frozen
Bokhara roses ...
And then the blur of snow. Time to be gone.

PHILIP LARKIN

Church Going

Once I am sure there's nothing going on
I step inside, letting the door thud shut.
Another church: matting, seats, and stone,
And little books; sprawlings of flowers, cut
For Sunday, brownish now; some brass and stuff
Up at the holy end; the small neat organ;
And a tense, musty, unignorable silence,
Brewed God knows how long. Hatless, I take off
My cycle-clips in awkward reverence,

Move forward, run my hand around the font.
From where I stand, the roof looks almost new –
Cleaned, or restored? Someone would know: I don't.
Mounting the lectern, I peruse a few
Hectoring large-scale verses, and pronounce
'Here endeth' much more loudly than I'd meant.
The echoes snigger briefly. Back at the door
I sign the book, donate an Irish sixpence,
Reflect the place was not worth stopping for.

Yet stop I did: in fact I often do,
And always end much at a loss like this,
Wondering what to look for; wondering, too,
When churches fall completely out of use
What we shall turn them into, if we shall keep
A few cathedrals chronically on show,

Their parchment, plate and pyx in locked cases,
And let the rest rent-free to rain and sheep.
Shall we avoid them as unlucky places?

Or, after dark, will dubious women come
To make their children touch a particular stone;
Pick simples for a cancer; or on some
Advised night see walking a dead one?
Power of some sort or other will go on
In games, in riddles, seemingly at random;
But superstition, like belief, must die,
And what remains when disbelief has gone?
Grass, weedy pavement, brambles, buttress, sky,

A shape less recognisable each week,
A purpose more obscure. I wonder who
Will be the last, the very last, to seek
This place for what it was; one of the crew
That tap and jot and know what rood-lofts were?
Some ruin-bibber, randy for antique,
Or Christmas-addict, counting on a whiff
Of gown-and-bands and organ-pipes and myrrh?
Or will he be my representative,

Bored, uninformed, knowing the ghostly silt
Dispersed, yet tending to this cross of ground
Through suburb scrub because it held unspilt
So long and equably what since is found
Only in separation – marriage, and birth,
And death, and thoughts of these – for which was built
This special shell? For, though I've no idea

What this accoutred frowsty barn is worth,
It pleases me to stand in silence here;

A serious house on serious earth it is,
In whose blent air all our compulsions meet,
Are recognized, and robed as destinies.
And that much never can be obsolete,
Since someone will forever be surprising
A hunger in himself to be more serious,
And gravitating with it to this ground,
Which, he once heard, was proper to grow wise in,
If only that so many dead lie round.

PHILIP LARKIN

A Stone Church Damaged by a Bomb

Planted deeper than roots,
This chiselled, flung-up faith
Runs and leaps against the sky,
A prayer killed into stone
Among the always-dying trees;
Windows throw back the sun
And hands are folded in their work at peace,
Though where they lie
The dead are shapeless in the shapeless earth.

Because, though taller the elms,
It forever rejects the soil,
Because its suspended bells
Beat when the birds are dumb,
And men are buried, and leaves burnt
Every indifferent autumn,
I have looked on that proud front
And the calm locked into walls,
I have worshipped that whispering shell.

Yet the wound, O see the wound
This petrified heart has taken,
Because, created deathless,

Nothing but death remained
To scatter magnificence;
And now what scaffolded mind
Can rebuild experience
As coral is set budding under seas,
Though none, O none sees what patterns it is making?

PETER LEVI

Shobdon

Out of the sight of God and his judgement
on Shobdon's Gothic stage the risen sun
gleams through the dead men's glass: God is content
to stream like light among us while no one
misunderstands his gentleman's accent.
In all the small hills there is no work done
but by severe seasons or with head bent,
as a bird sings, for small reward or none,
our gospel in our life's re-enactment,
our dying souls as saintly as a nun
flitter moth-like around fine ornament
like an expiring hour-glass whose sands run
slowly away till with the dying light
the season passes and the bone is white.

HERBERT LOMAS

Christ Church

Christ Church stands with black pricked ears
and clocks among the dripping trees.

I take the back lane down the worn stone steps
between the church and the sooty black trees.

The church has blackening angels in its graveyard.
The vicarage is where the murders were.

But inside there are gold-speared wrought-iron gates,
a gold cross parked on the choirstalls,

lights, a reredos and music. I walk into an orchestra
of violins, trumpets, flutes and bassoons,

and out of a scratchy old record of
'Hear My Prayer' and 'Angels Ever Bright and Fair'.

HERBERT LOMAS

St Martin-in-the-Fields

City churches aren't always easy
to pray in: there may be someone buffing up brasses
pianissimo, insistently, with cheesy
breath and a polish of rage behind their glasses,
sending almost tangible meditations
to distract our straggly congregations.

Or visitors delicately boggle at the faithful patients,
Guide Book in hand, not expecting religion
in architecture like this. Outside, the pigeons
drop little pats of white on assembled nations;
inside we pray, uneasily wondering:
whoever it is up there, is he listening?

Yet here bums in a blue-chinned Greek-looking worshipper,
pockets stuffed with evening newspapers, coat
flapping, and grabs his God by the throat:
he prays precipitately, wagging his head – a pew-gripper
pointing out to an old employer – what?
Is it horses? A tip flopped? A reproach or not?

And suddenly I'm in it: his grace has snatched
me out: over the altar the angels' faces
break the wood: they're reaching down with fact,

listening, embracing, swooping, and I'm hatched:
a broad white shell of completeness
has widened and cracked:
I'm open to sweetness.

ROLAND MATHIAS

Brechfa Chapel

Not a shank of the long lane upwards
Prepared our wits for the myth, the slimed
Substantiation of the elements. And the coot
With his off-white blaze and queasy paddle
Was an old alarm, the timid in flight
From the ignorant. The lowered shoulder
Of mountain it is, dabbled within the collar,
That shallows and darkens the eye, the first
Slack argent losing the light as bitterly
As the blackened water treads and nibbles
The reeds and bushes afloat in the new
Pool's centre. Beyond, a surviving ray
Points and fondles a reed-knot, the swan
That dreams on it taking no note of stumps
Or visitations. Nearer, however, and shifting
Like pillagers from weed to shore, settling
And starting raucously, hundreds of testy
Black-backs utter their true society, bankrupt
Hatred of strangers and bully unrest whichever
Marge they think themselves forced to. It
Is a militant brabble, staked out by wind
To the cropped-down pasture. Mud and the tricky
Green of the edge contrivingly clap it round
What's left of this latish day that began with love.

Opposite, to the west of the harsh lagoon,
Stands a chapel, shut in its kindred wall
With a score of graves. Legend on one
Cries a minister, dead of the heats in Newport
Before he came twenty-eight, his wife
Rambling on to her eighties. On another a woman
Loosens at thirty, her man afield on the mission
Ploughing till dark. O these stones trouble
The spirit, give look for look! A light from this
Tiny cell brisked in far corners once, the hand held
Steady. But now the black half-world comes at it,
Bleaks by its very doors. Is the old witness done?
The farmers, separate in their lands, hedge,
Ditch, no doubt, and keep tight pasture. Uphill
They trudge on seventh days, singly, putting
Their heads to the pews as habit bids them to,
And keep counsel. The books, in pyramid, sit tidy
On the pulpit. The back gallery looks
Swept. But the old iron gate to the common,
Rusted a little, affords not a glimpse
Of the swan in her dream on the reed-knot
Nor of the anxious coot enquiring of the grasses.
The hellish noise it is appals, the intolerable shilly-
Shally of birds quitting the nearer mud
For the farther, harrying the conversation
Of faith. Each on his own must stand and conjure
The strong remembered words, the unanswerable
Texts against chaos.

HUBERT MOORE

Crossing the Church

Some seem born to it. They could cross
the gleaming track from the nave to the altar
blindfold.

Look, no hands even. Now they're squaring
their shoulders eastwards, gravely inclining
their heads;

and now they're over, strolling off amidst pews,
leaving one at least of us standing
helpless

as ever to help the children we were,
who anyway couldn't be helped,
born

trespassers, laying our ears
to the cold steel of the track, hearing
the rail

singing the song that we hoped for,
five miles off, centuries still
for us,

knees bare on the flinty stone,
heads where the wheels would be rolling –
then scrambling safely across.

ANDREW MOTION

For Now

In the mind's eye, in the memory-store, for now
The church sets sail but stays where it was built,
Its anchor hooked into the parish-heart.

In the green yard, in the deep grass, for now
Each summer-tide swells up and leaves the dead
Untouched inside their plots of tilted earth.

In the flint nave, in the window-shafts, for now
The glassy saints grow limber with the sun
That ripples through their robes and walk again.

In the blind vault, in the dry hush, for now
The coffins hoard their argosies of dust
And darkness gleams as definite as light.

In the slow years, in the centuries, for now
The villagers arrive to load the ark
That saves their lives and settles here as home.

NORMAN NICHOLSON

Of this Parish

Here on the churchyard hill the dead lie higher
   (Under the winter
   Heliotrope, the garish
   Wreaths, the slanter
   Two o'clock shadow of the spire)
Than all the tall electors of this parish.

Not in the ore that fed them or the slate that sheltered,
   But in brown smoulder
   Of glacial clay
   The dead burn colder;
   While rain and tears are skeltered,
Down through the drains of the town to the sump of the bay.

We dump the wreaths in a ventilated bin:
   Soused in paraffin –
   Tulips, chrysanthemums,
   Premature blossoming thorn,
   Find in the flames
A short cut to the Resurrection Morn.

JOHN ORMOND

Cathedral Builders

They climbed on sketchy ladders towards God,
With winch and pulley hoisted hewn rock into heaven,
Inhabited sky with hammers, defied gravity,
Deified stone, took up God's house to meet Him,

And came down to their suppers and small beer;
Every night slept, lay with their smelly wives,
Quarrelled and cuffed the children, lied,
Spat, sang, were happy or unhappy,

And every day took to the ladders again;
Impeded the rights of way of another summer's
Swallows, grew greyer, shakier, became less inclined
To fix a neighbour's roof of a fine evening,

Saw naves sprout arches, clerestories soar,
Cursed the loud fancy glaziers for their luck,
Somehow escaped the plague, got rheumatism,
Decided it was time to give it up,

To leave the spire to others; stood in the crowd
Well back from the vestments at the consecration,
Envied the fat bishop his warm boots,
Cocked up a squint eye, and said, 'I bloody did that.'

PETER PORTER

An Angel in Blythburgh Church

Shot down from its enskied formation,
This stern-faced plummet rests against the wall;
Cromwell's soldiers peppered it and now the death-
  watch beetle has it in thrall.

If you make fortunes from wool, along
The weeping winter foreshores of the tide,
You build big churches with clerestories
  And place angels high inside.

Their painted faces guard and guide. Now or
Tomorrow or whenever is the promise –
The resurrection comes: fix your eyes halfway
  Between Heaven and Diss.

The face is crudely carved, simplified by wind;
It looks straight at God and waits for orders,
Buffeted by the organ militant, and blasted
  By choristers and recorders.

Faith would have our eyes as wooden and as certain.
It might be worth it, to start the New Year's hymn
Allowing for death as a mere calculation,
  A depreciation, entered in.

Or so I fancy looking at the roof beams
Where the dangerous beetle sails. What is it
Turns an atheist's mind to prayer in almost
   Any church on a country visit?

Greed for love or certainty or forgiveness?
High security rising with the sea birds?
A theology of self looking for precedents?
   A chance to speak old words?

Rather, I think of a woman lying on her bed
Staring for hours up to the ceiling where
Nothing is projected – death the only angel
   To shield her from despair.

PETER PORTER

At Whitechurch Canonicorum

This is a land of permutating green
and can afford its pagan ghostly state.
Only from the recurring dead between
the well-dark hedge and talking gate
can mystery come, the church's graveyard,
where now the sun tops the stones and makes
shadows long as a man work as hard
to live as he did, rotting there till he wakes.

That he will wake to trumpets they believed
or tried to who bought him ground to hold.
His dead eye takes in the high coiffure of leaves,
the pebble-dash tower, the numbers in gold
upon the clock face. For once he has reason –
this undistinguished church, whose frown
lies in the lap of Dorset rebuking each season
its appropriate worldliness, has a saint, pale and home-grown.

St Candida, white in her Latin and cement tomb,
has lived here since rumour was born.
A woman's pelvis needs only the little room
of a casket to heal the flesh it was torn
from: an enlightened bishop lifted up her lid

and pronounced her genuine, a lady's
bones who if she healed as they say she did
I ask to help me escape the further elbowing of Hades.

I tried to put once, while no one was about,
in the holes for the petitioners' limbs,
my love-starved body, for fear and doubt
not impotence, and spoke to that air which held hymns
like amber from the stained-glass sides
a prayer to the saint to be given love
by the person I loved. That prayer still resides
there unanswered. I gave the iron-studded door a shove

and stood again among the unsaintly dead.
St Candida is also St Wite,
the Latin derived from the Saxon misread,
the death clothes she sings in as bitter
to her as when her saintly heart stopped.
England has only two saints' relics confirmed
and hers are one. Three times now I've dropped
by at Whitechurch and asked her her easiest terms

for assistance. The old iron trees tend to roar
in the wind and the cloud seems unusually low
on the fields, even in summer. The weight of before
stands here for faith; so many are born and go
back, marvellous like painting or stones:
I offer my un-numinous body to the saint's care
and pray on my feet to her merciful bones
for ease of the ulcer of feeling, the starch of despair.

PETER PORTER

The Rider Haggard Window, St Mary's, Ditchingham

Time which eats the stories of our lives
Preserves a cruel freshness here to show
How energetic certainty contrives
To tell us what we think we almost know:
The warlike God of England will bestow
At least in retrospect on loyal wives
A school apotheosis, dirge of knives,
With dying, quick in life, in glass made slow.

A dubious transfer this, as history cools,
An ancient trespass, but a change of rules.
The world was opening which today is closed,
And where the mind went, destiny would tread
With God and Science noisily opposed
And story-telling garlanding the dead.

NEIL POWELL

At Little Gidding

for Matthew Desmond

1

In one hand Eliot, in the other Pevsner:
And yet we have arrived here unprepared.

2

Outside the farmhouse, a removal van
Announces a more permanent arrival:
Those clean cream walls seem inappropriate;
New settlers upset the visitor.

3

But not the church, which has seen worse than this:
Scrubby bushes, grey pock-marked façade
Proclaim a calm more honest and more modest,
God's domesticity.

4

     The scale is human.
Thus, quizzically, you rightly say you find
The tombstones more impressive than the church.
Grandeur was never Nicholas Ferrar's style;
His, the potent blend of craft and creed.

5

Not that this is Nicholas Ferrar's church.
It is his spirit's church; his church's spirit
Inhabits the carved ceiling of the chancel,
Informs the space beneath.

6

We sign the book.
Something you had not guessed had yet begun
Is completed in this ritual: the place
Belongs to us now; we are part of it.

7

Lifesize, it will stay with us as token
Of the size a life should be: it questions,
And Pevsner's words, not Eliot's, reply,
'Little Gidding is a confusing church.'

8

Only respect transcends confusion. Yes,
In the end, we were impressed. Deliberately,
We close the door, for birds are troublesome
(A notice tells us) and this church is loved.

9

Leighton Bromswold: 'Wonderful,' says Pevsner;
But we have no taste for it today.

NEIL POWELL

Iken

At Iken Cliff the well-fed tourists gather;
caravans, ice-cream, parodies of pleasure

drifting irresistibly towards Cliff Reach
where moody children mope at the muddy beach;

and none thinks to seek for solitude downstream
where, framed by trees, St Botolph's church awaits them,

gaunt and roofless, unthatched by fire and storm.
Decay has overtaken the postcard charm:

creepers in the tower challenge the bell-ropes;
a builder's sign recalls diminishing hopes

outside in the weed-choked churchyard. Iken lies
ruined at last after thirteen centuries,

echoes the collect for its founder: 'efface
we pray Thee the scars of our wounds and heal us.'

NEIL POWELL

Leiston Abbey

Ranulf de Glanville, Robert
de Ufford, your legacies
have weathered this rough climate
half-a-dozen centuries:
more potent, more angular
than you could imagine, your

second abbey stands among
the worshipping fields of grain,
as if the North Sea had flung
its whole weight upon the plain,
leaving these crags eroded
like relics on the sea bed.

A meeting of ages: near
the coast the power station
eyes the chapel at Minsmere
in silent confrontation
across the marshland which shields
sanctuary among wheatfields.

NEIL POWELL

Providence

The Providence Baptist Chapel, Aldringham,
Is light industrial: factory for souls,
Abandoned among heather, fern, and gorse,
Where birches lean their leaves against the wind,
It prompts old questions. Why here? Why at all?
I half-admire that monstrous confidence,
Unthinking certainty of doing good,
Which dumped a bumptious bright-red pantiled barn
Out here, far from community and road.
Now broken-windowed, boarded and patrolled
(It says) by ghostly guard-dogs, Providence
Has fallen out of use.

                                   Young oaks surprise
And jostle through the rusted graveyard fence.
The loyal congregation, being dead –
Adah Cadey, Sam Studd, Jabez Bird –
Worship in green, while yellow daisies dance
Upon the grave of Percy Marjoram,
Tended with love's defiance.

                                   I walk on,
Along a sandy track, a silent lane:
New planting, like a wartime cemetery
Or rockets poised for launch on Guy Fawkes' Night,
Proclaims the future forest's greener hope;
And a neat brick row of charitable homes

Shows how goodwill can be inhabited
As peace of mind, as warmth.

                                Yet faith runs cold.

A sign outside the Baptist Chapel said:

Black Horse Agencies (Subject to Contract) SOLD.

RODNEY PYBUS

Suffolk Church

God, this obdurate desire
to endure:

these flint-congested walls
are solid marvels the years
can't take much more of;
mottled and dashed from earth
to roof and hopeful spire,
they must once have seemed
short roads to heaven, cobbled love.

Now these flints like lumps of bone
take the relic stains of air,
darkening brown and white and grey;
perhaps once well-built prayers
that lost their way congealed to stones
just right for setting hard
this hand-made aggregate of God.

VICKI RAYMOND

Boveney Church

Ahead in the mist, a squat church
has suddenly appeared,
like a bully lying in wait
at the edge of the tow-path.

An old fighter, it seems,
for the souls of bargees.
A blunt twelfth-century tower
shapes up to the Thames.

The river at this point
is not festive. The odd fisherman
hunches in oilskins and pipesmoke
among reeds. The church, of course,

is locked. I peer through a slot
and make out some beams,
the end of a pew, hymnals
and prayer books. The usual glimpse.

If I should ever forget
myself so far as to marry,
and in church too, it might
well be a church like this one:

so suited to departures
into regions of mist, so flint-faced
in promising so little
and expecting even less.

PETER READING

St James's

On Holy Thursday cycling in the Lakes
I found St James's on a pewter hill
and force of habit rather than desire
carried me on towards the wrought iron gates.

The dusty Dunlops and the worn out brakes
of my Rudge leaning on the lake-stone wall
seemed more akin to Larkin than to me.

Some stones inside the musty porch were Saxon,
and there, beside the patent-leather Eden
simmering round St James's in Lent sun,
the sexton, one spring day digging a grave,
in 1898 unearthed remains
that proved to be of Viking origin.

The latest stone, marked 1968,
shews that the process is still going on.
I, in my turn, turned the worn rusting latch,
saw the inevitable Norman arch
and, near the font, some notes by Reverend Twigge
about the church and local history –
he was the rector here in nineteen seven,
in his place now is Geoffrey Dennison Hill.

I climbed the old steps up the Western Tower
(added about 1248) and found
barrows of sticks from jackdaw generations,
piled in a stook beside the swaying bell
eggs and dry feathers and winged skeletons,
and I descended into the chancel,
observing, not from interest but a sense
of having to have a sense of history,
the aimless woodworms' doodles in the roof.

The empty Player's *Weights* pack in the font
belonged to Betjeman, I have no doubt,
and there was Larkin's shilling left in trust
as payment for the Reverend Twigge's epistle;

but I was not there, just a cardboard copy
guiltily going through the motions of
what all day-trippers do before they leave,
replacing bike clips, lingering at the door
giving the closing latch a final twist,
consulting Twigge one final time before
turning from font to underground stone kist.

ANNE RIDLER

Edlesborough

Beyond the Chiltern coast, this church:
A lighthouse in dry seas of standing corn.
Bees hive in the tower; the outer stone
Pared and frittered in sunlight, flakes with the years:
Clunch crumbles, but silence, exaltation endures.

The brass-robed Rector stretched on his tomb endures.
Within, we go upon the dragon and the bat,
Walk above the world, without,
Uplifted among lavender, beech and sycamore,
Shades of the sea-born chalk, indelible and austere.

If we see history from this hill
It is upon its own conditions, here
Each season swirls and eddies the circle of a year
Round the spectator church, and human eyes
Take, on its plinth, a long focus of centuries.

We seem like gods on any hill.
From here all toil resembles rest, and yet
Unlike a god we feel ourselves shut out.
Surely that farm in a carved blue curve of trees,
So still with all its creatures, holds the unattainable peace?

It is Time's camouflage deceives us.
There it extends like space: whatever moves

(A horse to drink, a reaper to stack the sheaves)
Displays the movement in its whole succession,
Not a change of terms, only a changed relation.

Deceit or truth? The dead possess the hill
In battlements of totternhoe or slate;
The view is ours, the range and ache of sight.
Their death, our life, so far apart, unite
If Time serves: in a common space unrolls
This Resurrection field, with sheaves in glory like risen souls.

VERNON SCANNELL

In a City Churchyard

It is quite small, no necropolis, this;
A hamlet of mortality, a place
For specialists to visit, library
Of lithic manuscripts displayed on green,
Or what might once have been before the long
Urban plague, grey death, had withered it.
Only three students have come here today:
Old lady, shuffling past in canvas shoes
Attached to unimaginable legs;
Old man who sleeps in methylated peace;
A mongrel dog who studies with his nose
Then lifts an indolent leg to make
Brief annotation on a mossy page.
No one else, unless we should include
The solitary stone angel who attends,
Despite the little insults of the birds
And mottling pox of weathers on its skin,
The promised day when trumpet-calls proclaim
Eternal holiday of white on green,
Take-off for grounded angels who may see,
From glorious perch of sunbeam or star's wrist,
Rejuvenated lady, dancing dog,
The sleeping drinker's dream corporified.

DAVID SCOTT

Locking the Church

It takes two hands to turn the key
of the church door, and on its stiffest days
needs a piece of iron to work it like a capstan.
I know the key's weight in the hand
the day begins and ends with it.
Tonight the sky is wide open
and locking the church is a walk
between the yews and a field of stars.
The moon is the one I have known
on those first nights away from home.
It dodges behind the bellcote
and then appears as punched putty or a coin.
The key has a nail for the night
behind the snecked front door.
Carrying a tray of waters up to bed
I halt a careful tread to squint
through curtains not quite met
at the church, the moon, and the silver light
cast on the upturned breasts of the parish dead
locked out for the night.

PETER SCUPHAM

Dissolution

Recall now, treading the cloister garth's clipped grass,
That time the Commissioners urged their sweating horses
About the uneasy land. Under huge gates they paced,

Ironically savouring that final confrontation,
The long concessions leading to surrender.
Houghton, Whiting: some took martyrdom. To fresh vocations

Most adjusted, leaving the cool painted house
Of prayer, and all its various furniture,
Each known and local contour of a dwelling place.

Lead bubbled, wood-smoke ascended. Rough secular hands
Fluttered both text and commentary, levelled well-set courses
Of cut stone for manor, mansion. God made no visible amends.

A spectacular pleasure, some. Bolton to the suave Wharfe leans
Her vacant choir. From Crowland's screen, decaying features
Gaze severely at the unlettered town.

Such emblems landscape bears as sands bear shells:
Twinned tokens, disciplines where life declines.
In an attentive ear, the same far rumour swells.

PETER SCUPHAM

Minsden

The chapel bears this press of trees,
Leading old windows, topping out
Some roof above the fallen roof,
Bustling their heavy green about
The shrouded flint. A pallid breeze
Picks at the twigs and faded stuff,
Fussing the tangled floor: dust blurs
Lost village and lost villagers.

Life here without her facing stones
To rule and quarter out the sky.
Only the pleated crunch, a spill
Of light poured off rough drapery
As blacks and whites and ochre tones
Work shifts about the curtain wall.
Ground shakes to sun; the rough infill
Glimmers about the nave and chancel

Where history, historian lie,
Recorded and recorded dead;
His granite flake split, slewed across,
Dark table for a sunburnt head
Of votive flowers: the twist and tie
Of chamomile, corn, scabious.
Black flint secretes a fuller shade:
Cool gold strikes out across the glade.

PETER SCUPHAM

Rule

Freshets of rain: in such a glister
Decay speaks with her Roman tone;
God's City lies in scattered chapters,
The warm bread broken into stone.
    Eve passes with her basket; was
    Learned deeply here in bells and grass.

On features limned by Towne or Crome,
The ivy wanders à la mode:
An Early English style, appointed
To recollect us to our God.
    Light, where the foliaged waters run,
    And cattle lodged on gleams of sun.

The County History trails its blazons,
Bound in the tenantry's cowed skin;
Armorial in dissolution,
The Western sky looks full, yet thin.
    Sir Priest, in Tennysonian bands,
    Lies chancelled into folded hands.

Amen. The loose leaf of a Psalter
Glosses in gold our primal sin,
The ways we went through fire and water.
Those reds and blues embroidered in

The hammered uncials lose their threads,
A tangled harness for beast heads.

The power is stated, spent, retained:
Old Lear, Victorian with bright eyes,
Is bearded in his den with flowers.
John Gilbert's rough calligraphies
    Work out new crowns of thorn, entwine
    Cordelia as Columbine.

The Rector's horse is beautiful;
The Curate's jade is picturesque.
A disenfranchised demon wears
His runnelled face in sour grotesque,
    A conduit for the tumbling skies.
    We feel the water-table rise,

Staining the vellum signatures,
Parting the mason's greening seam;
The arks of our lost covenant
Beach out on Ararats of dream
    In rain which congregates the night
    Across such breadth, and from such height.

PETER SCUPHAM

Service

Hearing the organ stray,
Wambling slow time away
In sit and stand,
A candle-bracket cold to hand,

Watching the shadows pass
Under this burning-glass:
One bright eye
Of lapis lazuli

Over an old saint's head,
A running maze of lead.
Robes of blood,
And little understood

But the high lancet's blue
Which makes the whole tale true
And is definite,
Shifting its weight of light

As afternoon lies dying,
The trebles following,
Stone gone dim,
God down to his last hymn.

PETER SCUPHAM

Stone Head

The tower so clearly made of light,
The loneliness of light, from lonely money
Sighed away on a late medieval death-day,
And the pretty names: mouchettes, sound-holes,
Double-stepped battlements with pinnacles –
One of God's fairy things

To sway with clouds, but pinned
Into the illusion of a high motion, lift-off,
Setting four devils at their platform angles
Reaching for Heaven, crop-winged
For fear of flying: saturnine,
Staring themselves out of countenance.

Till slam. After so much star and cloud
A thunderbolt of wind cracked off the corner
And flung this one poor clone of Lucifer
Headlong. Picked from couch-grass,
His down-to-earth bone-glare
Domesticated in a red-brick alcove,

He has put off the smell of brimstone:
One of the Foliots, Lares, Genii,
'That kinde of Devils conversing in the earth',

As James puts it in his *Demonologie*.
Lop-eared, crook-mouthed, cheek-chapped,
Kissing-cousin to Meg Merilees.

The Longaevi, the fallen angels:
One down, and three to go,
To suffer jolt and jar or slow erosion.
Look in the grass; find his bolted feet
Still clawing for a toehold
On a flawed block of consecrated stone.

JON SILKIN

The Cathedral Chair

Of a skip: of a monument
of hollowed burned space; outside which,
   brayed rubble.

With buttress
and saint air takes shape. The skip holds
   a chair,

its swivelled
body quietly nesting, whose tubby grandeur
   carts

to the knacker's.
Without murmur; the arch-bishop's diurnal
   track slid

about this swivel
on God's terse demands, or between
   a man's buttocks.

So gently
I lift this thing, and I strip away
   rexine

buttons
and the soiled studs, and, in ounces,
   the tattered mullions of leather

and the wool
until the wood frame in its muslinned flesh
    – it glimmers,

it is a god peeled. I give this figure
skin, and sit cupped,
in its thinking the idea sepalled

of the most dear absences, and which
unfolds in the ventricle of lithe air.

C.H. SISSON

In Kent

Although there may be treacherous men
Who in the churchyard swing their mattocks
Within they sing the *Nunc Dimittis*

And villagers who find that building
A place to go to of a Sunday
May accidentally be absolved

For on a hill, upon a gibbet...
And this is Saint Augustine's county.

C.H. SISSON

Knole

The white hill-side is prickled with antlers
And the deer wade to me through the snow.
From John Donne's church the muffled and galoshed
Patiently to their holy dinners go.

And never do those antlered heads reflect
On the gentle flanks where in autumn they put their seed
Nor Christians on the word which, that very hour,
Their upturned faces or their hearts received.

But spring will bring the heavy doe to bed;
The fawn will wobble and soon after leap.
Those others will die at this or the next year's turn
And find the resurrection encased in sleep.

C.H. SISSON

Muchelney Abbey

The quiet flood
Lies between hedges and turns back the light,
Black and blue like the bruises of the time
– Sheet after sheet of record where the crime
Is lost beneath the water. Rushes write
Illegibly in mud

And willows point
Downward without weeping, or else raise
Flourishing heads topping gigantic trunks.
Uneasily the shadows of dead monks
Move past an abbey in which no-one prays.
Who will anoint

The wounds they did not,
More than we do ourselves, attempt to cure?
Grey evening behind which the sun, unseen,
Sets to the sound of church-bells, which still mean
No more than echoes: and, for sure,
Nature will rot.

O come away
To death O human race! Accept no more
This watery world in which the fox and hare
Have lost their scent, in which the livid air

Promises nothing on this wasted shore
But closing day.

Yet spring may come,
Who knows? with drought and terror, or else flowers,
For time may circle back, once more pretend
A grammar of renewal without end,
A summer with its vacuum of bright hours.

JON STALLWORTHY

At the Church of St John Baptist, Preston Bissett, May 1974

Dear John, if a sinner may so
address a saint in his own house,
I come, as others about to go
on a journey have come to these
worn steps, through seven centuries,
to ask a blessing, make their vows,
and look for assent, a sign from your window.

Here they received the names that are
all that remain of them, brown ink
in a parish register,
a shadow on lichened stone:
and among those lifelines, my own.
It draws me outside to the brink
of their graves and it draws me further.

Let me go down to them and learn
what they learnt on their journeys.
And in the looted cavern

of the skull, let me restore
their sight, their broken speech, before
from these worn steps or steps like these
speechless to the speechless I return.

ANNE STEVENSON

Pennine

Hills? Or a high plateau scissored by rivers?
Strong as grass, a winter's crop of stones
Craters the drive. The black paths trickle.
Randomly, fells erupt in armoured cliffs
That might be houses – might, in this cloud, be
Slack, grit, slag, moss, a memory of mills.

Everything trains to the perpendicular.
Trees stand taller on one green root than another.
The village is slabbed like steps into its slope,
The churchyard paved with graves, thronged with unbalanced
Mitred headstones, an asylum of bishops. The dead
Are unsafe. Their graves hardly hold them.

Victorian conscience breathes over church and ruin
A slatey rain. Whoever sent a dove
To star the cross where Thomas Holinrake's buried
Guessed that its message needed marble.
Feathers and blood stab at the lichened walls,
Stonefalls crossing in their long decline.

SEÁN STREET

Churchyard

August day,
English evening

yew trees.

A maze of table tombs'
eroding stone.

Yew trees.

Old stone
carvings fading to fog,

Words gone far from their dead thought,
defeated by lichen.

Show me some sign. What point
is a grave without a message?

Here's just
a faint angel, man-made.

SEÁN STREET

Knowlton, Cranborne Chase

The fallen church deconsecrates
forgotten ritual with a broken cross.
Something shared bridges millennia –
ruin within ruin, one wrecking the other.

From all around the ghosts come to die,
hanging leafy heads, drifting in
from Badbury and Ackling Dyke –
relics over which their congress broods.

It is not strange that the hill turns away,
refusing our further persuasions,
for it has renounced its own phantoms,
thrown all past life to Win Green's winds.

KIM TAPLIN

Fairford Windows

Wealthy John Tame five hundred years ago
had this church built out of Cotswold sheep.
We cannot see it as they saw it then:
dirt and lichen dim the coloured windows,
soften the brash conviction; jumbled leads,
botched cracks, blurred lines and time have made obscure
the story of the faith in images,
'the Bible of the poor'.
Yet they survived;
figures on glass fragile as flesh is frail,
somehow disarming Puritan rage,
removed and hidden in 1939 from unimpassioned bombs.

Our modern weapons leave no time for that,
nor any hearts to write the story on.
Stiff-necked sightseers we go the round,
sipping the colours like wine,
trying to make out the disfigured face of God.

First light.
In the garden.
Theft of knowledge.
The green tree spoiled.
Eve and the Tempter look alike.

Second light.
Moses on holy ground.
Revelation.
Gift of knowledge.
The green tree burns uneaten ...

Speaking likenesses, knowable people,
Eve in the garden, Moses, Mary,
Joseph, Pilate, Peter, Thomas,
Matthew, Mark, Isaiah, David,
Augustine, Solomon, Judas, John.
And among the rest John Tame's wife Alice
kneels trustingly close by her risen Lord;
and beyond the open tomb the River Coln
winds its familiar way through Gloucestershire.

Mediaeval art has made the Doom too tidy.
We cannot see it as they saw it then.
We have conceived a child we dare not know
– no red devils, no blue devils – mankind,
whose crawling flesh gapes at itself in terror.

We do not know whether that man was God;
but words that are not made flesh are merely idols,
peace, freedom, justice, *caritas*, truth;
and as we know that what we do
threatens his likenesses,
so we know ourselves judged
as the sun streams gold through the west window
by this one who sits upon a rainbow
with our world at his wounded feet.

R.S. THOMAS

The Belfry

I have seen it standing up grey,
Gaunt, as though no sunlight
Could ever thaw out the music
Of its great bell; terrible
In its own way, for religion
Is like that. There are times
When a black frost is upon
One's whole being, and the heart
In its bone belfry hangs and is dumb.

But who is to know? Always,
Even in winter in the cold
Of a stone church, on his knees
Someone is praying, whose prayers fall
Steadily through the hard spell
Of weather that is between God
And himself. Perhaps they are warm rain
That brings the sun and afterwards flowers
On the raw graves and throbbing of bells.

R.S. THOMAS

Country Church

(Manafon)

The church stands, built from the river stone,
Brittle with light, as though a breath could shatter
Its slender frame, or spill the limpid water,
Quiet as sunlight, cupped within the bone.

It stands yet. But though soft flowers break
In delicate waves round limbs the river fashioned
With so smooth care, no friendly God has cautioned
The brimming tides of fescue for its sake.

ANTHONY THWAITE

At Dunkeswell Abbey

Below the ford, the stream in flood
Rises and laps the leaf-choked wood
And fallen branches trap thick mud.
Pebbles are swept like slingstones down
Runnels and channels sliced through stone
And in the hollows sink and drown.

On either side broad ramparts hold
The water back from copse and field,
Where a dry earthbank seems to fold
Protectively a hollow space
Of pasture edged with stunted trees
In its inert and curved embrace.

Six hundred years ago, great pike
Grown old in this man-fashioned lake
Swam through its lily clusters like
Dream-presences below the mind.
Dark waters stirred where now I stand
Hearing the distant stream unwind.

The stillness here was made to last.
Whatever shapes survive exist
In some faint diagram of the past,
A sketch-map tentative as those

Robbed walls whose simulacrum lies
In patches summer droughts expose.

One wall still overtops the trees
Beyond the ford, but bramble grows
Round rotten stone. What energies
Persist are harnessed to the stream,
Violent in flood, not curbed or tame,
And hurtling without plan or aim.

ANTHONY THWAITE

At Dunwich

Fifteen churches lie here
Under the North Sea;
Forty-five years ago
The last went down the cliff.
You can see, at low tide,
A mound of masonry
Chewed like a damp bun.

In the village now (if you call
Dunwich a village now,
With a handful of houses, one street,
And a shack for Tizer and tea)
You can ask an old man
To show you the stuff they've found
On the beach when there's been a storm:

Knife-blades, buckles and rings,
Enough coins to fill an old sock,
Badges that men wore
When they'd been on pilgrimage,
Armfuls of broken pots.
People cut bread, paid cash,
Buttoned up against the cold.

Fifteen churches, and men
In thousands working at looms,

And wives brewing up stews
In great grey cooking pots.
I put out a hand and pull
A sherd from the cliff's jaws.
The sand trickles, then falls.

Nettles grow on the cliffs
In clumps as high as a house.
The houses have gone away.
Stand and look at the sea
Eating the land as it walks
Steadily treading the tops
Of fifteen churches' spires.

ANTHONY THWAITE

Eccles

Cliffs sifting down, stiff grassblades bent,
Subdued, and shouldering off thick sand,
Boulders – compacted grout and flint –
Jut from a stranded beach, a land
Adhering thickly to the sea.
Tide-drenched, withdrawn, and drowned again,
Capsized, these buttresses still strain
Towards perpendicularity.

The place-name mimes the fallen church,
Abbreviated, shrunk to this
Truncated word, echo of speech,
A Latin ghost's thin obsequies
Carried by wind, answered by sea –
Ecclesia: the syllables
Curtailed, half heard, like tongueless bells
From empty steeples endlessly.

ANTHONY THWAITE

Manhood End

At Manhood End the older dead lie thick
Together by the churchyard's eastern wall.
The sexton sweated out with spade and pick
And moved turf, clay, bones, gravestones, to make room
For late comers, those whose burial
Was still far off, but who would need a tomb.

Among the pebbles, in the molehills' loam
Turned thighbone up, and skull: whatever frail
Relic was left was given a new home,
Close to the wood and farther from the sea.
Couch-grass grew stronger here and, with the pale
Toadstools and puffballs, masked that vacancy.

In April, on a day when rain and sun
Had stripped all distances to clarity,
I stood there by the chapel, and saw one
Lean heron rising on enormous wings
Across the silted harbour towards the sea.
Dead flowers at my feet: but no one brings

Flowers to these shifted bodies. The thin flies,
First flies of spring, stirred by the rain-butt. Names
Stared at me out of moss, the legacies
Of parents to their children: *Lucy, Ann,*

Names I have given, which a father claims
Because they mean something that he began.

Cool in the chapel of St Wilfred, I
Knelt by the Saxon wall and bowed my head,
Shutting my eyes: till, looking up to high
Above the pews, I saw a monument,
A sixteenth-century carving, with the dead
Husband and wife kneeling together, meant

For piety and remembrance. But on their right
I grasped with sudden shock a scene less pure –
A naked woman, arms bound back and tight,
And breasts thrust forward to be gnawed by great
Pincers two men held out. I left, unsure
Of what that emblem meant; and towards the gate

The small mounds of the overcrowded dead
Shrank in the sun. The eastern wall seemed built
Of darker stone. I lay: and by my head
A starling with its neck snapped; nestling there,
A thrush's egg with yolk and white half spilt,
And one chafed bone a molehill had laid bare.

Frail pictures of the world at Manhood End –
How we are shifted, smashed, how stones display
The names and passions that we cannot mend.
The lych-gate stood and showed me, and I felt
The pebbles teach my feet. I walked away,
My head full of the smell my nostrils smelt.

ANTHONY THWAITE

The Mole at Kilpeck Church

Fierce kicks and thrustings under turf and leaf
Reveal you, revenant,
Still lively under so much buried grief,
So ready to be quick when all are dead,
So plucky in extending your dark head
Among the carvings of the lost and spent.

Even that famous randy lady who,
Spreading her swollen thighs,
Enacts in stone the acts that we would do,
Seems nothing to your rushing push, your flair
For room to breathe when all the churchyard air
Shrinks to a mere frame for your energies.

ANTHONY THWAITE

Reformation

The hazed meadows of England grow over chancels
Where cattle hooves kick up heraldic tiles
And molehills heap their spoils above slumped walls.
The cruck-beamed roofs of refectories nestle under
Sheds and barns, hay piled high where
Augustine and Aquinas chapter by chapter
Were read in these now lapsed pastoral acres.

Small streams wash the smashed crockery of Cistercians.
Stone-plaited carvings are wedged in gable ends
Of farmhouses, springs irrigate robbed chapels
Where all is marsh, reeds meshed among cracked altars.
A buzzard shrieks *yaa-i* in a tall tree.
Plainchant echoing along the valleys.
High hedges stand above spoiled finials.

And Sunday mornings see small meeting houses,
Reformed parishes and tabernacles,
Bethesdas and the whole wide countryside,
All split seven ways in sect and congregation,
Assembling to praise God from whom all blessings
Flow through his derelict priories, abbeys, cells
The afternoon sun will show, faint shadows among fields.

ANDREW WATERMAN

Ludham, St Catherine's Church, The Rood Screen

For those who gave to make what's here,
Intricate carved wood, tracery,
Pinnacled buttresses, *in the year*
Of ower Lord God MCCCCLXXXXIII,

The middle rail of folded leaf
Is inscribed: *Pray for the sowle*
Of John and Cycyly his wyf
And *alle other* … Centuries roll

Over what this hammerbeam
Roof sequesters. Civil fights,
Broad-brims with the zealot's dream
To beat out Popery's stained lights.

Still clear the colouring of those
Depicted on the rood screen's base:
St Edmund, St Walstan, St Ambrose –
And here St Appolonia's face,

Patron of dentists, with drawn tooth
In forceps ... Perpendicular
Stonework clinches fossil truth
Outflanked by video, motor car.

Empanelled dead saints gather dust,
With faith in means whereby they bless;
Yet swell me to what feels like trust,
Winging unsure of its address.

ROWAN WILLIAMS

Please Close This Door Quietly

The slow, loud door: pushing against
a mound of dust, dust floating
heavily in a still room; step
slowly,

Stones can deceive. The ground looks
firm, but the dust makes you blink
and feel for purchase. This is
marshland,

Difficult light to sting eyes, terrain
whose spring and tangle hides deep
gaps, cold pools, old workings;
careful.

Too much left here of unseen lumber
dropped, knowingly or not, behind
the door to trip you while you rub
awkwardly

At naked eyes, opened on thick,
still, damp, scented air, imprinted,
used and recycled, not clearing up;
catching:

The weather of memory. Underfoot
lost tracks wind round an ankle
and abandoned diggings, wells, mines,
foundations,

Wait for your foot to find them,
drop you into the unexpected chill,
the snatched breath and swift
seeing,

The bird's flap at the edge
of your eye's world: things left
but alive; a space shared; a stone
yielding.

CLIVE WILMER

East Anglian Churchyard

The land low-lying – the fen drained –
Still partakes of the flood, and the soil
Of this green graveyard still has the swell,
The broken swell, of a calm sea, beneath which
Graves are submerged.

And this church – dateless, its wall at a lean
And no tower – is a beached ship,
Perhaps of northern pirates who having no more
Rich coastal abbeys to fire, settling,
Passed from the blue.

From the deep half-salvaged, there is one tombstone
That rears above the surface where leaf-light swims
In the shade of an oak-tree, ageless, ivied –
The stone entwined by the same ivy, its name
Blotted by moss.

Beside recent deaths, no other stone
In sight – though here and there, a vague swell
Covers a forgotten life. This
Particular spot in the shade, he must have
Chosen for memory.

CLIVE WILMER

Near Walsingham

Springs rise where saints have prayed,
  Tradition says;
 And tells of rivulets and wells
  Conceived of rumoured deities.

But streams would have obeyed
  No peremptory hand.
 Where water has already blessed the land
  Saints choose to pray.

Gods walk when glint and spade
  Strike, as it brims,
 A buried watercourse. One dreams
  A cryptic meaning for the source:

Meaning which haunts the shade
  That falls by bridge and ford,
 Lodged in the thought and speech that harken toward
  The interminable

Tale given and not made
  Or understood,
 Which haunts the place. What we might say
  Of what it tells would speak of God.

CLIVE WILMER

The Ruined Abbey

And now the wind rushes through grassy aisles,
And over the massy columns the sky arches.

The monks who built it
Were acquainted with stone and silence.
Knowing the grandeur and endurance
Of isolated winter oaks, of rock,
And the hard rhythms of moors,
They retired here and reared it
From the crust of the north, moulding this form
Around their core of silence.

Their minds were landscaped.
Not with summer gardens that give sense ease
Nor beaches that lull questionings to a doze.
Their landscapes asserted agonies that
Probed them to the nerve;
The hardness of rock and the stream's ice
Formed a resistance they learned to resist,
To subdue, till it yielded
To silent movements of joy –
To the penetrating warmth of a mellow sun,
Its venerable eye.

The streams locked by ice,
The rocks, and the edged wind
Resisted their cowled will to define.
But resistance tautened questionings whose sinew
Shaped understandings.
The moor's silence snowed meanings,
And they knew that, while ice melts or cracks, they
Could endure like the rocks.

And so from the stone of landscaped minds, they fashioned
A form for those meanings, a form
That arched over meaningful air.
According to their time they shaped it
With massive grace.
And in the face of evil, weathers and decay
Its essence constant in the shifting of ages.

And now the wind rushes through the grassy aisles,
And over the massy columns the sky arches.

In ruin, the form remains;
When the form falls, there is stone;
Stone crumbled, there is still
The dust, dust … and a silence
The centuries bow to – a silence
Lapped by the speechless howl of winds.

ANDREW YOUNG

The Ruined Chapel

From meadows with the sheep so shorn
They, not their lambs, seem newly born
Through the graveyard I pass,
Where only blue plume-thistle waves
And headstones lie so deep in grass
They follow dead men to their graves,
And as I enter by no door
This chapel where the slow moss crawls
I wonder that so small a floor
Can have the sky for roof, mountains for walls.

Gazetteer

EXPLANATORY NOTE

The following churches are all referenced directly or obliquely in this anthology, and the relevant poets are named in parentheses following the parish name. Almost every poem in this collection is inspired by a specific church. A few seem to describe a specific building, as in Larkin's 'Church Going' and Pybus's 'Suffolk Church', but are in fact amalgams. Some of the poems are amalgams of two or three churches that can be identified, such as Wilmer's 'The Ruined Abbey' and Scupham's 'Rule' and 'Dissolution', and in such instances I have included entries on all the sites to which these poems allude. Some poems, such as Thwaite's 'Reformation', Sisson's 'In Kent', Jennings' 'Somerset', Cavaliero's 'Fenland Churches', Greening's 'A Huntingdonshire Nocturne' and Hill's 'Loss and Gain', describe a host of churches in general terms, or an ecclesiastical region, and do not allude to specific, individual churches. Other poems, such as Garfitt's 'Rites of Passage', Crossley-Holland's 'In Latter Days' and Silkin's 'The Cathedral Chair', describe church furnishings, the prayer book or other ecclesial features rather than a specific church. In some instances, such as Grigson's 'West Window', Young's 'The Ruined Chapel' and Larkin's 'A Stone Church Damaged by a Bomb', I have been able to make a fairly reliable ascription as to the church referenced. In others the specific church remains tantalisingly out of reach. Such is the case with Scannell's 'In a City Churchyard'. The poem was written not long after his move to Canterbury, where he lived and taught at the King's School. Scannell's churchyard could quite possibly be that of St Alphege's Church, now redundant and part of the King's School, but there are many old churchyards in Canterbury that he might have visited, and thus the particular site has eluded me.

Aldringham, Providence Baptist Chapel (Powell) Designed by Cecil Howard Lay and opened in 1915, replacing an earlier chapel erected in 1812. Built to serve the Particular Baptists, now converted to a private residence. Aldringham is 3 miles NW of Aldeburgh on the Suffolk coast.

Ayot St Lawrence, St Lawrence (Scupham) Two parish churches here, a Norman ruin and a neoclassical temple that holds services once monthly. The original was partially demolished in 1775 and turned into a 'Gothick' ruin. The parish church is on a Palladian design of Nicholas Revett. The confluence of styles partly inspired the poem 'Rule'. In Hertfordshire, 30 miles N of London.

Blisland, St Protus and St Hyacinth (Causley) Mostly 12th century construction, with 15th century barrel-vaulted ceiling with carved angels. Modern touches by F.C. Eden include pulpit, windows, rood screen and rood loft. In the words of Betjeman, Blisland 'is a living church whose beauty makes you gasp, whose silence brings you to your knees'. Remains a thriving Anglo-Catholic parish. In Cornwall, 36 miles NW of Plymouth.

Blythburgh, Holy Trinity (Porter) Massive 15th century church, informally known as the 'Cathedral of the Marshes', rising out of Suffolk's Blyth estuary. A dozen majestic carved wooden angels survive in the ceiling, too high for 17th century iconoclasts to destroy. Superb bench ends depict the seven deadly sins, the seven works of mercy and the labours of the seasons. Still an active parish. 29 miles SE of Norwich.

Bolton Abbey, Priory Church of St Mary and St Cuthbert (Scupham, Wilmer) Founded 1154 by Augustinians and mostly completed by 1170. The nave, which serves as the local parish church, survived the Dissolution and is the only part of the abbey not in ruins. Victorian restoration, including windows by Augustus Pugin. Remains an active parish. In the Yorkshire Dales, 17 miles W of Harrogate.

Boveney, St Mary Magdalene (Raymond) A redundant church dating from the 12th century, built to serve bargemen working the nearby Thames and functioning as chapel-of-ease to Burnham St Peter. Constructed of flint and chalk rubble, with 15th century weatherboarded tower and a simple vernacular interior. Under the care of the Friends of Friendless Churches. Near Eton, approx. 2½ miles W of Windsor.

Brechfa, Bethesda Chapel (Mathias) Nonconformist chapel built in 1803 in superb scenery on the banks of Brechfa Pool, now a vital sanctuary for numerous bird species. In 1920 skulls of horses were discovered in the ceiling, placed there out of either a misguided notion about acoustics or a vestigial paganism. Now converted to a private residence. Near the village of Llyswen, Carmarthenshire, 31 miles N of Swansea.

Cambridge, King's College Chapel (Betjeman) The finest example of English Perpendicular Gothic architecture. Contains the largest fan-vaulted ceiling in the world. The massive Italianate rood screen, supporting the central organ case, stands in marked contrast to the chapel's other features. Twelve massive stained-glass windows decorate each side of the chapel. Rubens' *The Adoration of the Magi* decorates the altar. Famed for its choral services.

Cambridge, St John the Evangelist (Scupham) A lively and thriving parish founded in 1891. Constructed in redbrick Victorian gothic and lit, as 'Service' indicates, by extraordinary east and west windows. Stands opposite Homerton College at the southeastern end of Cambridge.

Carlton, St Peter (Wilmer) An austere and diminutive fieldstone building. Nave walls are 12th century; fittings date mostly from the 14th and 15th centuries. As 'East Anglian Churchyard' suggests, it is towerless and its east wall leans precariously. Sir Thomas Elyot is buried in the churchyard. Still a functioning parish. 15 miles SE of Cambridge.

Charfield, St James (Fanthorpe) Dating from the 13th century but largely rebuilt in the 15th. Stone rubble walls and Cotswold slate roof. The crenellated tower is also saddlebacked. Unrestored interior is largely medieval. Churchyard contains memorials to 15 people killed in the 1928 Charfield railway disaster. Redundant, and in the care of the Churches Conservation Trust. 7 miles N of Chipping Sodbury, Gloucestershire.

Cheetham Hill, St Mark (Connor) Founded in 1794 in what was then a hamlet in Lancashire but is now an inner-city ward of Manchester. In the 19th century, Cheetham Hill began to attract large numbers of European immigrants and was heavily urbanised; its large Jewish population expanded rapidly in the 20th century with immigrants from around the world. The church closed in 1982 and was later demolished. Nothing remains besides the gates, railings and gravestones in its churchyard.

Church Norton, Chapel of St Wilfrid (Thwaite) The tiny chapel of St Wilfrid (also spelled 'Wilfred') stands on the site of the first cathedral in Sussex, in the area of Church Norton known locally as 'Manhood

End'. The gruesome carving the poem describes is of the martyrdom of St Agatha. Half of the building was dismantled in 1860 and moved to Selsey to expand the church there. Declared redundant in 1990 and now in the care of the Churches Conservation Trust. 8 miles N of Chichester.

Coventry, Cathedral Church of St Michael (Larkin) Of 14th and 15th century construction, and one of the largest parish churches in England when elevated to cathedral status in 1918. Bombed in the Coventry Blitz on 14 November 1940. The shell survives, and serves as the entrance pavilion to the new cathedral designed by Basil Spence, which opened in 1962.

Cranbrook, St Dunstan (Moore) Known informally as the 'Cathedral of the Weald'. Largely late medieval construction. Tower has three extraordinary Green Men dating from around 1300. Carved wooden figure of Father Time above the tower clock. Unusual 18th century font designed for full immersion. Thriving parish, in Kent, 14 miles S of Maidstone.

Crowland, Abbey Church of St Mary the Virgin, St Bartholomew and St Guthlac (Scupham) Founded in the 8th century and came under Benedictine Rule in the 10th century. Monastic buildings destroyed in the Dissolution, but the nave survived and continues to function as the parish church. Said to be the first church in England to have a tuned peal of bells, dating from AD 986. The pull is the longest in England. In Lincolnshire, 9 miles NE of Peterborough.

Ditchingham, St Mary (Porter) Late 15th century church set away from the village in open Norfolk countryside. Massive west tower visible for miles. Famous for its stained glass, including a memorial window to the author of *King Solomon's Mines*, a former churchwarden. Remains an active parish. 15 miles SE of Norwich.

Dunkeswell Abbey (Thwaite) Founded 1201 by Cistercians. Demolished following the Dissolution. Holy Trinity, Dunkeswell Abbey was built over the site of the cloisters and nave in 1842, in the Early English Style. Parish in decline and services held only on occasion. In East Devon, 33 miles SW of Yeovil.

Duntisbourne Rouse, St Michael (Horovitz) An ancient but still active Cotswold parish. The nave is of Saxon origins and the chancel is Norman, with a saddleback tower and herringbone stonework. 13th century chancel paintings survive. Other features include 15th century misericord grotesques, Jacobean pulpit and Victorian box pews. Duntisbourne Rouse is in Gloucestershire, about 4 miles NW of Cirencester.

Dunwich, All Saints (Thwaite) The last of Dunwich's 15 churches to be swallowed by tidal erosion on the Suffolk coast. Heavy coastal flooding in the 13th and 14th centuries began the process, and All Saints was abandoned by the 1750s. The cliff edge reached the church's nave in 1904, and in 1922 the west tower collapsed into the sea. Ruins of the 13th century Greyfriars Priory survive in Dunwich, 33 miles SE of Norwich.

Eastwell, St Mary the Virgin (Fuller) Constructed in the 15th century at Eastwell Park, the country house of the earls of Winchilsea. After the roof collapsed in 1951, the shell was demolished, leaving intact only the tower and the south wall. The village of Eastwell is about 4 miles N of Ashford, Kent.

Eccles-on-Sea, St Mary (Thwaite) The ruin of a ruin, located in the former village of Eccles-on-Sea Norfolk. Village and church were both abandoned by the 19th century. The tower stood until 1895, and all ecclesiastical rubble is now inundated by sand and tide. 20 miles NE of Norwich, on the Norfolk coastline.

Edlesborough, St Mary the Virgin (Ridler) Perched atop a barrow in the Aylesbury Vale in Buckinghamshire. Of mostly 14th century construction, with 15th century rood screen, pulpit and misericords. Numerous interesting brasses. Declared redundant in 1975. Now under the care of the Churches Conservation Trust. 37 miles NE of Oxford.

Fairford, St Mary (Grigson, Taplin) Large, beautiful and exceptionally well preserved 15th century church, built with the wealth of the Gloucestershire wool trade. Nearly perfect example of English Perpendicular. Superb choir screens and extraordinary misericords. Contains spectacular 15th and 16th century stained glass of the highest quality. Its glorious west window is of the Last Judgement, with Satan depicted as Leviathan carrying the damned to Hell. Active parish, 29 miles W of Oxford.

Feltwell, St Nicholas (Cavaliero) Original 7th century church partly demolished and rebuilt about 1070. Aisles and clerestory added in 15th century. Six flushwork panels decorate the clerestory's south side. Chancel and tower demolished in the 19th century, rendering the nave as wide as it is long and giving it the appearance of a barn outside and that of a meeting-house inside. Large, clear windows create a well-lighted interior. Declared redundant in 1973 and now under the care of the Churches Conservation Trust. On the edge of the Fens in SW Norfolk, 19 miles NE of Ely.

Fountains Abbey (Ashby, Wilmer) One of the largest and best preserved monastic ruins. Founded by Cistercians in 1135. Much of the building was completed by 1170. Closed in 1539 during the Dissolution. Owned by the National Trust and operated by English Heritage. In North Yorkshire, 3 miles SW of Ripon.

Freshwater, All Saints (Hinton) One of the oldest churches on the Isle of Wight and with a still functioning parish. Partly Norman but greatly restored in the 19th century. Contains memorials to Alfred, Lord Tennyson. The churchyard, edging the Yar Estuary, contains the grave of Lady Tennyson and their son Hallam. The lych gate was imported from nearby Mottistone Church. 27 miles E of Bournemouth.

Glastonbury Abbey (Scupham) Founded in the 7th century, rebuilt in the 12th century. Until the Dissolution it was one of the richest and most powerful monasteries in England. The ruins have been designated a Scheduled Ancient Monument, and it remains a site of religious pilgrimage. Persistent Arthurian associations make it a popular tourist destination. In Somerset, 27 miles S of Bristol.

Glencorse, Old Kirk (Young) Of medieval origins, extensively rebuilt in the 17th century. R.L. Stevenson had close associations with the kirk. Abandoned after the construction of new parish church in 1883, and soon thereafter the roof fell in. This picturesque Church of Scotland ruin was recently 'rescued' and re-roofed, and now serves as a wedding venue. In Midlothian, 8 miles S of Edinburgh.

Glendalough, Priory Church of St Saviour (Davie) 12th century Augustinian priory. Buildings demolished during the Dissolution, but many fine and distinct architectural and decorative features remain visible in the Romanesque ruins. In County Wicklow, Ireland, 32 miles S of Dublin.

Great Hampden, St Mary Magdalene (Adcock) Rebuilt in the 14th century, and modified through the ages. Notable features include early 16th century pews, a 15th century piscina, late 13th century lancets, and 16th century bells still in use. Numerous monuments and brasses to members of the Hampden family, including leading 17th century Parliamentarian John Hampden (remembered in Gray's 'Elegy Written in a Country Churchyard'). Still a thriving parish. Located in Buckinghamshire, 6 miles N of High Wycombe.

Greensted-juxta-Ongar, St Andrew (Fanthorpe) Oldest wooden church in the world and the only example of a Saxon timber church. Most of the nave is original, dating to the 7th century; the brick chancel is 14th century. The body of Saint Edmund, King of East Anglia, lay in state in Greensted Church in 1013 on its way to Bury St Edumuds. Still an active parish. 13 miles W of Chelmsford, Essex.

Heptonstall, St Thomas à Becket and St Thomas the Apostle (Hughes, Stevenson) Heptonstall's 13th century 'old church', now a ruin though occasionally used for services, is dedicated to Becket; the new church, dedicated to the apostle, was consecrated in 1854 and remains an active parish. Contains some fine stained glass and a Lady Chapel. Burial place of Sylvia Plath. Near Hebden Bridge in West Yorkshire, 27 miles NE of Manchester.

Houghton Saint Giles, Chapel of St Catherine of Alexandria (Henry) Known informally as 'Slipper Chapel'. Final stop on route of medieval pilgrims to the shrine of Our Lady of Walsingham. Built in 1340; fell into disuse after the dissolution of the monasteries. Was used as a barn until 1896, when it was restored and donated to Downside Abbey. Consecrated in 1934 as the Roman Catholic National Shrine of Our Lady. In Norfolk, 25 miles NE of King's Lynn.

Huttoft, St Margaret (Betjeman) 13th century limestone, with Saxon tower and Victorian restorations. Interior carvings include gargoyles, human head corbels and foliage sprays. Fine 15th century octagonal font. 20th century painted reredos and carved rood screen. Parish in decline but Sunday services still held. On the Lincolnshire coast, 39 miles E of Lincoln.

Iken, St Botolph (Powell) Thatched-roof building, distinguished for its historic embodiment of Anglo-Saxon Christianity and its spectacular setting on Iken Cliff overlooking the Alde estuary. Nave is 12th century, the tower 15th century and the chancel 19th century. Near the font is a section of a 9th century cross with dragon biting its own tail. Occasional services still held. On the Suffolk coast near Aldeburgh, 20 miles NE of Ipswich.

Kidderminster, St Mary and All Saints (Hill) Largest parish church in Worcestershire, and still thriving. Founded 12th century though existing building is mostly 16th century. Some Victorian renovation. Beautiful stained glass, ornate tombs and monuments. The Puritan controversialist Richard Baxter was one of its most famous preachers, giving his first sermon here in 1641. On the banks of the River Stour in central Kidderminster, 19 miles SW of Birmingham.

Kilpeck, St Mary and St David (Adcock, Thwaite) Constructed around 1140 in local red sandstone. Its nearly perfect Norman features were untouched by Puritan reformers or Victorian restorers. Noted for its remarkable corbels depicting both Christian and mythological images, the latter of which include green men, a manticore, a basilisk and the famous sheela-na-gig grotesquely exposing her genitalia. An active Herefordshire parish, near the Welsh border, 10 miles SW of Hereford.

Knowlton (Street) A Norman ruin of unknown dedication, built in the 12th century and surrounded by a Neolithic earthen henge. The church was abandoned in the 18th century when the roof collapsed. Situated on the chalk plateau of Cranborne Chase, 7 miles N of Wimborne Minster, Dorset.

Leighton Bromswold, St Mary the Virgin (Powell) Of 14th century origins, but in a ruinous state by the 17th century. Substantially rebuilt by poet and priest George Herbert, whose first ecclesial living this was. The altar and nave seating are owing to Herbert's designs, as are the twin oak reading and preaching pulpits, the chancel screen and the choir stalls. A still active Cambridgeshire parish, 5 miles S of Little Gidding and 30 miles NW of Cambridge.

Leiston Abbey (Powell) Founded 1182 by Augustinians. Present ruins, demolished in the Dissolution, date from 1363. The original ruins, 2½ miles N, became the site of Minsmere Chapel, now also in ruins. Leiston is now in the guardianship of English Heritage. In Suffolk, 26 miles NE of Ipswich.

Little Gidding, St John the Evangelist (Greening, Powell) Diminutive church with great cultural significance. Deep associations with the Anglican religious community of Nicholas Ferrar and poet George Herbert, and memorialized by Eliot in *The Four Quartets*. Nave is 13½ feet wide and can hold only 30 worshippers. Present structure rebuilt in 1714. Font, lectern and communion table are original to Ferrar's occupancy. Evensong held periodically. In Cambridgeshire, 14 miles SW of Peterborough.

Little Staughton, All Saints (Greening) Formerly dedicated to St Margaret. Well-proportioned tower and steeple. Crenellated nave dates to 13th century, chancel and tower to 15th century. Medieval decoration, furnishings, statues and stained glass all destroyed during Reformation. Contemporary vandals have attacked spire, roof and drains. When Huntingdonshire lost its county status, this active parish became part of Bedfordshire. 25 miles W of Cambridge.

Llandaff, Cathedral Church of St Peter, St Paul, St Dyfrig, St Teilo and St Euddogwy (Ormond) Present cathedral, dating from 1107, stands on one of the oldest Christian sites in Great Britain. Stunning west front rebuilt 1220. The roof and much of the interior was destroyed in the Second World War, and the present interior is a sensitive blending of ancient and modern. Altar contains triptych by D.G. Rossetti, and the reinforced-concrete chancel arch has Sir

Jacob Epstein's aluminium statue of Christ in Majesty. In the Llandaff Conservation Area of Cardiff, Wales.

Llantrisant, St Peter, St Paul, and St John (Cluysenaar) Celtic origins, but rededicated after Norman Conquest. Present building is largely 14th century, with Victorian restoration. 17th century scissor-rafter roof in nave. Outsized battlemented tower dwarfs nave and chancel, giving new meaning to 'church militant'. Active parish near Usk, Monmouthshire, 24 miles NE of Cardiff.

London, St Martin-in-the-Fields (Henry, Lomas) A neoclassical monument on Trafalgar Square, rebuilt 1722–4 by James Gibbs. Its notable features include a Corinthian portico and elegant spire, a barrel-vaulted nave and graceful plasterwork. Famous both for its mission to aid the homeless and its musical programmes, it remains a thriving parish.

London, St Saviour, Aberdeen Park (Betjeman) A masterpiece of the Arts and Crafts movement, completed 1865. Built as a refuge for the Anglo-Catholics of North London. Remarkable patterned brickwork walls, mosaics, ironwork and encaustic tiles. Declared redundant in 1981. Now the home of the Florence Trust studios. Located in the Highbury district of Islington.

Ludham, St Catherine (Waterman) Built during the prosperous medieval wool trade in the Norfolk Broads. Tower and chancel are 14th century; nave is 15th century. Fine hammer-beam ceiling. Spectacular rood screen of 1493 survived the predations of the reign of Edward VI. A thriving parish, 14 miles NE of Norwich.

Luss, St MacKessog (Crichton Smith) Church of Scotland parish, founded *c.* 510. Present building dates from 1875. Cruciform Decorated Gothic with belfry at crossing. Central pulpit and lovely stained glass. Picturesque setting on Loch Lomond, in Argyll. Active parish and site of Christian pilgrimage. 26 miles NW of Glasgow.

Manafon, St Michael and All Angels (Thomas) Simple 13th century rectangle with slate roof. Single chamber containing nave and chancel. Victorian 'restoration' introduced Anglo-Catholic interior features to this simple Welsh construction as well as lych gate. Timbered belfry holds a single bell dating from early 14th century, still rung. Poet R.S. Thomas was rector from 1942 to 1954. Remains an active Anglican parish in the Church in Wales. In Powys, 29 miles SW of Shrewsbury.

Marsden, St Bartholomew (Armitage) Extraordinary Victorian gothic designed by a pupil of Sir George Gilbert Scott. Contains fine stained glass and mosaic floors, and a peal of ten bells. Informally known as 'the Cathedral of the Colne Valley'. A lively and active parish. Marsden is 7 miles SW of Huddersfield.

Millom, St George (Nicholson) Built in the 1870s atop a hill. Its towering spire, with gabled buttresses, is visible for miles. Contains memorial window to Norman Nicholson, who was confirmed here in 1940 and is buried in the churchyard his poem commemorates. Still an active parish. In Cumbria, on the edge of the Lake District, 70 miles NW of Preston.

Minsden, St Nicholas (Scupham) Abandoned chapel-of-ease formerly tied to Hitchin St Mary in Hertfordshire. Used by pilgrims on route to St Alban's Abbey. Fell into disuse following the Reformation and became a ruin by the eighteenth century. The tomb is that of Reginald Hine, a solicitor and local historian who took his own life in 1949. 30 miles SW of Cambridge.

Minsmere, St Mary (Powell) Aka Minsmere Sluice Chapel, and now a preserved ruin. Built on the site of the ruins of the original Leiston

Abbey following its move 2½ miles S in 1363. Demolished along with the abbey in the Dissolution. Site used as defence against coastal invasion in WWII. In East Bridge, 29 miles NE of Ipswich.

Montacute, St Catherine (Fanthorpe) Of 12th century origins, the church was extensively restored by Victorian architect Henry Hall. One of its vicars was the Reverend Charles Francis Powys, father of the three Powys brothers who all became writers. Remains an active parish. Montacute is in Somerset, about 4 miles W of Yeovil.

Muchelney Abbey (Aykroyd, Sisson) Site contains ruins of Anglo-Saxon abbey, medieval Benedictine abbey and 16th century Tudor house. Abbey buildings demolished in the Dissolution. Ruins adjacent to the still active 15th century parish church of St Peter and St Paul, Muchelney. Its ceiling contains Jacobean paintings of bare-breasted angels. In Somerset, 11 miles NW of Yeovil.

New Milton, St Mary Magdalene (Heath-Stubbs) An unlovely early redbrick Victorian church built on medieval foundations in the section of town now known as Old Milton. The tower, squat and crenellated, is 17th century. Still an active parish. Situated on the edge of the New Forest near Christchurch Bay, 13 miles E of Bournemouth.

Ormside, St James (Reading) Well-preserved 11th century Lake District church with interior Norman arches and font. Gabled west tower added in 13th century. In 1823 an Anglo-Saxon cup, the 'Ormside bowl', was discovered in the churchyard, and in 1898 a Viking warrior and his sword were uncovered. Remains an active parish. In the Eden Valley, 36 miles SE of Carlisle.

Painswick, St Mary (Street) Of late medieval origins, most famous for its churchyard with its 99 clipped yew trees and its tabletop tombs. One of the few Anglican parishes where the ancient custom of 'clipping the church' is kept alive. Church tower has a ring of 14 bells and an active bell-ringers' society. Tower has bullet scars from English Civil War. In the Cotswolds, 7 miles SW of Gloucester.

Penarth, St Augustine (Clarke) Victorian Gothic in Early English style by William Butterfield. Replaced a ruined medieval church the parish had outgrown, still active today. Brilliant polychromatic brickwork interior, encaustic tiles and ribbed ceiling. 90 foot saddleback tower. Its prominent hilltop position, visible from great distances, has given it the affectionate nickname of 'Top Church'. Situated on Penarth Head, at the SW tip of Cardiff Bay, 4 miles S of Cardiff.

Pendomer, St Roch (Day-Lewis) A small fieldstone church of 13th century origins, in scenic hilltop setting. Its limited features include a Norman font and nondescript 18th century tower. A mere 2½ miles from East Coker, where T.S. Eliot is buried in the church he memorialised. A very small but still active parish, nestled between Crewkerne and Yeovil in Somerset, 47 miles S of Bristol.

Preston Bissett, St John the Baptist (Stallworthy) Mostly 14th century construction, with squat 12th century tower. Octofoil clerestory added to heighten the nave in the 19th century. Lovely reticulated windows with flowing tracery. A living parish. In Buckinghamshire, about 24 miles NE of Oxford.

Roche, St Gomonda (Clemo) 15th century tower, but the rest of the church dates from 1822. Fine Norman font. Remains an active parish. Nearby are a holy well and Roche Rock, with deep associations in legend and folklore, and a ruined chapel on its top. In Cornwall, 20 miles NE of Truro.

Runham, St Peter and St Paul (Scupham) Primarily of 14th century construction, and brutally restored in the 19th century. A gothic-fantasy tower, with corbels and spectacular pinnacles, was the work of local architect J.T. Bottle. Fell into disuse in the 1970s and became derelict, then restored and reopened in 2007. An all-too-rare success story. Near Mautby, Norfolk, 17 miles E of Norwich.

St Hilary, St Hilary (Causley) Founded in the 13th century, but only the tower is original. Following a fire in 1853, the church was rebuilt in the Early English style. St Hilary is important in the Cornish Anglo-Catholic movement, and after its interior was damaged by Protestant vandals in 1932, the chancel was redecorated with the work of Newlyn School artists. The reredos was painted by Roger Fry. Parish is part of a thriving united benefice. The village of St Hilary is located on the southern Cornish coast, 6 miles E of Penzance.

Sevenoaks, St Nicholas (Sisson) Dating from the 13th century, though partly rebuilt in the 15th century. Parish church serving Knole House, the country estate of the Barons Sackville and the Earls and Dukes of Dorset. John Donne served as rector from 1616 to 1631. A vibrant parish in the evangelical tradition. In Kent, 20 miles W of Maidstone.

Shobdon, St John the Evangelist (Levi) An unrestored Georgian masterpiece, with 13th century tower. Its ornate white interior and furnishings embody the most perfect example of 'Strawberry Hill Gothick', the blend of Rococo and Gothic briefly popularised by Horace Walpole. An active parish, Shobdon is in Herefordshire, about 8 miles W of Leominster.

Stisted, All Saints (Motion) Thriving parish near Braintree, in Essex. Chancel is 13th century, clerestoried nave is 14th century. East wall of chancel has five graduated lancets. 19th century tower has unusual broach spire, resembling a witch's hat. 14 miles W of Colchester.

Thurgarton, All Saints (Barker) A redundant church dating from the 14th century. Constructed with flint walls and thatched roof. The interior is notable for its original medieval benches, whose ends are carved with such figures as musicians, animals and mythical beasts. Under the care of the Churches Conservation Trust. Situated 20 miles N of Norwich, near the Norfolk coast.

Todmorden, Christ Church (Lomas) Large Gothic revival, opened in 1832. A stained-glass window commemorates the Rev. Anthony John Plow, who was murdered at the vicarage in 1868, along with one of his servants. Declared redundant in 1992; now in private ownership and converted into a single-family residence. In West Yorkshire, 22 miles NE of Manchester.

Torpenhow, St Michael and All Angels (Scott) Built about 1120. One of a very few unspoiled Norman churches in England. Sandstone construction with green slate roof and open bellcote. Extraordinary chancel arch is carved with demons, animals and humans. Baroque nave ceiling is painted with cupids and garlands; it came from a London Livery Company as a gift from the brother of Joseph Addison in 1689. The poet was vicar here from 1980 to 1991. Thriving parish in Cumbria, 18 miles SW of Carlisle.

Towcester, St Lawrence (Curtis) Large ironstone parish church with Saxon origins. Current building is 12th century, with Early English, Decorated and Victorian embellishments. 90-foot tower added in 15th century contains a current ring of 12 bells. Two medieval paintings – one of a pelican in piety – survived the Reformation. Contains grotesques on the chantry arch and a rare cadaver tomb of a 15th century archdeacon. The poet's father was vicar here from 1953 to 1981. In Northamptonshire, 35 miles NE of Oxford.

Uffington, St Mary (Betjeman) Known informally as 'the Cathedral of the Vale'. 13th century cruciform construction of sandstone and a nearly perfect example of medieval ecclesiastical architecture. The spire was lost in a storm in 1740, but the octagonal tower is finely proportioned. The church has strong personal associations with authors Thomas Hughes and John Betjeman. Still in use. 21 miles SW of Oxford.

Walsham-le-Willows, St Mary the Virgin (Crossley-Holland) A still-active parish, largely 15th century church but with earlier portions. Impressive clerestory and east window. Spectacular roof of alternating tie-beams and hammer-beams; its decorative carved angels were removed by churchwardens on the orders of Henry VIII. In Suffolk, 13 miles NE of Bury St Edmunds.

Walsingham Priory (Wilmer) Ruins of a 10th century Augustinian monastery. Famous destination of medieval pilgrims for its Marian shrine. Monastic buildings destroyed during the Dissolution. Shrine Church of Our Lady of Walsingham rebuilt in early 20th century and is again a site of pilgrimage and devotion, in the Anglo-Catholic tradition. In Norfolk, 28 miles NW of Norwich.

Westwell, St Mary (Kavanagh) Small but lovely Cotswold church of Norman origins with Early English and Victorian modifications. Unique features include a sundial scored into the Norman south door serving as 'mass clock', a 12th century font, an unusual rose window and a 19th century bellcote. A living parish in Oxfordshire's Shill Valley. 22 miles W of Oxford and 16 miles NE of Circencester.

Whitechurch Canonicorum, St Candida and Holy Cross (Porter) Largely Early English and Perpendicular, with some Norman features. 12th century font and 15th century tower. 13th century limestone and marble shrine to St Wite (Latinized as Candida). The sole English parish church known to have retained intact the relics of its patron saint. Still holds regular services. On the west Dorset coast, 21 miles W of Dorchester.

Winchester, St Cross (Hooker) An ancient chapel within the parish of Winchester Cathedral and attached to the Hospital of St Cross and Almshouse of Noble Poverty. Founded in 1183. Its tranquil and beautiful Hampshire setting is matched by the cathedral proportions of the vast and well-preserved Norman chapel. Serves as chapel to the Brothers of St Cross, but its services are public.